LEADING
WELL

David Pich and Ann Messenger

First published in 2019 by Major Street Publishing Pty Ltd
PO Box 106, Highett, Vic. 3190
E: info@majorstreet.com.au
W: majorstreet.com.au
M: +61 421 707 983

The moral rights of the authors have been asserted.

Quantity sales. Special discounts are available on quantity purchases by corporations, associations and others. For details, contact Lesley Williams using the contact details above.

Individual sales. Major Street publications are available through most bookstores. They can also be ordered directly from Major Street's online bookstore at www.majorstreet.com.au.

Orders for university textbook/course adoption use. For orders of this nature, please contact Lesley Williams using the contact details above.

A catalogue record for this book is available from the National Library of Australia

ISBN: 978-0-6482387-7-5

Cover design by Principle Design
Internal design by Production Works
Printed in Australia by Ovato, an Accredited ISO AS/NZS 14001:2004
Environmental Management System Printer

10 9 8 7 6 5 4 3 2 1

Disclaimer: The material in this publication is in the nature of general comment only, and neither purports nor intends to be advice. Readers should not act on the basis of any matter in this publication without considering (and if appropriate taking) professional advice with due regard to their own particular circumstances. The authors and publisher expressly disclaim all and any liability to any person, whether a purchaser of this publication or not, in respect of anything and the consequences of anything done or omitted to be done by any such person in reliance, whether whole or partial, upon the whole or any part of the contents of this publication.

CONTENTS

Preface **v**

1. **Respect** 1
   David Pich and Jamie Getgood

2. **Integrity** 29
   Michelle Gibbings

3. **Emotional Intelligence** 59
   Susanne Behrendt

4. **Ability to Inspire** 97
   Sam Bell

5. **Authenticity** 127
   Allison Keogh

In Conversation 165
Interviews with five leaders who lead well

6. **Self-Awareness** 199
   Margot Smith

7. **Decisiveness** 227
   Bill Kernoczy and Luke Challenor

Lead Well. Go Chartered! **261**

References **265**

Index **272**

Join the Institute of Managers and Leaders **280**

PREFACE

There can be very little doubt that leadership matters.

In 2017, after working for three decades and across two continents in the leadership space – from human resources (HR) to marketing to senior management – I published my first book on leadership, *Leadership Matters – 7 skills of very successful leaders*. In it I wrote that I felt leadership success wasn't just about 'the inspiring', it was also very much about 'the doing'. *Leadership Matters* held that much of today's leadership theory, advice and thinking was focused on the 'inspiration' side of the equation, and the actual 'doing' – the tough stuff, the blood, sweat and tears of leadership – was too often ignored. It was ignored precisely because it was hard work. *Leadership Matters* was focused on the perspiration of leadership.

But what happens when leadership isn't based on inspiration? What happens when leaders don't at least ignite a little passion into those they lead? What happens when leadership is *all* perspiration – and no pzazz?!

A couple of years after *Leadership Matters* was published, I feel compelled to revisit the inspiration side of the leadership equation. By emphasising the importance of the practical, hands-on business of leadership, I wonder if I have inadvertently succeeded in implying that the inspirational side is simply the unimportant leadership fluff. Have I unintentionally led leaders to believe that they can be successful by 'doing' alone? I hope not, because this is certainly not the case.

Inspiration is the guiding star of leadership – it's what leaders aspire to and aim for, and it's the benchmark by which we measure our own success. Leadership success *isn't* achieved just by perspiration. Leaders can only achieve success with a unique balance of inspiration and perspiration. If perspiration is the rudder that guides leadership, inspiration is the North Star. It's the destination. It's the brightness that shines and keeps people on track.

I freely admit that I thought writing about the inspirational side of the leadership equation would be the easier of the two books to write. I thought that I had got the tough one out of the way by writing *Leadership Matters* first. However, it soon became clear that the problem with covering the inspiration side of leadership – unlike the hard skills – is that it tends to need to be personified by our personal leadership heroes.

Leadership inspiration is too often attributed to the idea of a leadership genius – one saintly figure who personifies all the virtues of leadership. Just a quick Google search of 'leadership inspiration' shows it often manifests as motivational quotes from the likes of Steve Jobs, Einstein or Gandhi – which, at first, doesn't make the idea of a genius leader sound terribly bad.

The problem with the concept of genius leaders, however, is that they don't always represent leadership. These often-glorified CEOs, politicians and philosophers sit on a pedestal where they're worshipped by us – the people who aspire to achieve their level of success. To thousands of emerging leaders around the world, these people are their North Star, but what happens when these leaders disappoint us?

What happens when Elon Musk leverages the misfortunes of a team of Thai boys trapped in a cave to create a kid-sized submarine for a PR stunt? What happens when Nobel Peace Prize laureate and beloved Burmese leader Aung San Suu Kyi refuses to condemn a state-sanctioned genocide against one million of her own people on the basis of their religion and ethnicity? What happens when hundreds of our on-screen heroes are revealed to have been abusing their power to commit horrifying acts of sexual violence?

People in leadership positions can make poor leadership decisions. When we believe in the concept of a leadership genius, we too easily overlook actions and attributes of poor leadership. If the news headlines of poor leadership over the past year have reinforced one thing, it's this: great leadership is never about one leader; it's the combined attributes of good leadership performed by leaders. Thus, *Leading Well – 7 attributes of very successful leaders* was born. It's a leadership inspiration book focused on *leadership*, not leaders.

I made the decision at the very start of the writing process to consult with the Institute of Managers and Leaders' (IML) 10,000 Members about the seven attributes that would form the basis of this book. Of course, finding consensus among such a diverse and experienced cohort was always going to mean that some attributes would be left out. Some Members were going to be disappointed and perhaps even disagree with the inclusion of some of the chapters in *Leading Well*.

In the interests of complete transparency, we asked IML's Membership to rank a total of 35 leadership attributes in order of importance. The seven that were selected for inclusion in this book were the top seven selected by our Membership – Respect, Integrity, Emotional Intelligence, Ability to Inspire, Authenticity, Self-Awareness and Decisiveness. The list isn't intended to be exhaustive – the seven attributes presented here are merely a starting point.

Obviously, this isn't a precise science. Once the results of the survey were in, it was very difficult to justify rejecting Passion when it received almost as much 'support' as Integrity. But that's life, and that's leadership! Leadership itself isn't an exact science. If it were, we'd all be great leaders all of the time, and we wouldn't need books like this to help us on our leadership journey!

Leading Well isn't intended to be inspiring (although, if it does inspire that's even better); it's intended to give you the tools to be inspired. This book doesn't tell you who or what to be inspired by, it shows you *how* to be inspired by leadership. Knowing how gives you the ability to grow into a great leader by learning from leadership's best attributes.

Leading Well isn't a book about inspiring leaders, it's about inspiring leadership. I hope you learn a little about how to inspire others and how to be inspired yourself.

Good luck and lead well – always.

David Pich
MA (Cantab), Chartered Manager, Fellow of the Institute
of Managers and Leaders
Chief Executive, Institute of Managers and Leaders

Chapter 1

RESPECT

David Pich and Jamie Getgood

Respect is how you treat everyone,
not just those you want to impress.

Richard Branson

Author note

On joining the Institute in 2015, I was well aware that I was joining an organisation with a long and proud history of promoting and recognising management and leadership excellence. With hindsight, I don't think I fully understood this at the time. It only really hit home when I hosted my first Leadership Excellence Awards event in October 2015. These Awards were designed to recognise great leaders across a number of management and leadership categories, and they had been part of the Institute's portfolio in one guise or another for more than 30 years.

In 2017 I had the privilege of presenting the Institute's 'Leader of the Year' Award to Jamie Getgood. It wasn't difficult to see why the eminent panel of judges had selected Jamie. He was (and remains), without doubt, an exemplary leader. What really stood out to me was Jamie's humility and personal code of ethics. For him, leadership is about 'walking the talk' and treating others as he would want to be treated.

Having heard a little about Jamie's leadership style and the way that he led and managed the difficult downsizing of the Holden manufacturing facility in South Australia, I jumped at the chance of co-authoring this chapter of Leading Well with him. Together we decided to tackle the tricky leadership attribute of Respect.

Respect is especially tricky because it is so hard to define.

In many ways it can feel as if the concept of respect in the workplace belongs to a bygone age; to a time when it was based more on your position in the hierarchy of the organisation than on anything you did for that organisation. Of course, times have changed and with that change has come a far broader definition of – and demand for – respect in the workplace.

Today's workplace reflects today's society. Our teams comprise people of all genders, sexualities, religions and races. Increasingly, today's managers and leaders are working in organisations and alongside colleagues from different countries, continents and cultures.

Respect is increasingly the key to organisational performance and to leadership success. This chapter looks at the elusive attribute of respect and offers insights into the ways that today's leaders can lead in a respectful and inclusive way.

GOOD LEADERSHIP AFFORDS the opportunity to make a significant difference to the vision, direction and expected outcomes of a business. But it's more than that. Good leaders can have a significant impact on the people they lead. This impact can be as immediate as it can be long-lasting. Indeed, while leadership done well has the ability to positively alter the culture and purpose within an organisation, increase output, enhance reputation and drive the bottom line, perhaps more importantly it can lead to improvements in the self-esteem and the character of the people being led.

Key to all of this is acknowledging that leadership is people-centred. It focuses on engaging the power of who we are at the deepest level. It is inclusive, empowering and reflective of our core values, and what we believe about our own identity, meaning and purpose. Where management is primarily focused on process, leadership is built, formed and developed beyond the processes – in the people.

Often when we step up to a leadership role for the first time, we have great plans and ideas about what leadership looks like and what we think will and won't work. We have typically armed ourselves with the latest theories, having read myriad text books and managerial guides on what makes a great leader, and we enter that brave new world relatively confident in our ability to lead well. In addition, because we've all had first-hand experience of the good, the bad and the ugly of leadership and of leaders in our past who have shaped and structured us into a certain way of thinking – both positive and negative – we reassure ourselves that we'll be fine.

Then Leadership Day 1 happens and we immediately dive directly into the strategy, systems and processes of our new department or business. We make our purpose and priority the analysis of how we can drive performance across our teams. We do this because we think *that's what leaders do.* Leaders get results, don't they?

This focus on systems and process lacks a vital element: respect. We can be a nice and sociable, knowledgeable and experienced manager, but if we are bound by process and don't work to gain and maintain the respect of our team, we will never achieve the best performance possible from them. Without respect, leaders are destined to remain as managers, focused on processes and systems and struggling to take that all-important step up to great leadership.

Respect is absolutely pivotal to good leadership. It differentiates a great leader from a manager. Respect is a value and this makes its delivery and acceptance diverse across people and culture. It is also an incredibly challenging attribute because it is a value that tends to be different for everyone. Often, it is a complexity of many different experiences, predisposed considerations, principles, cultural norms, behaviours, feelings and outcomes that can make it feel almost fluid and hard to pin down. This chapter of *Leading Well* will attempt to do just that.

DEFINING RESPECT

Sometimes when you're faced with an attribute that is likely to be slightly tricky to describe and work with, it's worth falling back on what might be considered to be an expert view. *The Oxford English Dictionary* defines respect as *'a feeling of deep admiration for someone or something elicited by their abilities, qualities, or achievements'* and further as, *'due regard for the feelings, wishes or rights of others'.*

While this definition is (as dictionary definitions do tend to be) rather broad, it does provide a solid starting point for considering respect as being a crucial leadership attribute. A slightly amended definition of respect, and one that I have come to view as being crucial to my own leadership journey, is to see respect as the ability to value and honour others, their words and actions, even if we do not ourselves share the same views.

I acknowledge that these two definitions diverge somewhat, but I think in the overlap the real power and essence of the attribute lies. Having 'due regard' for what others feel and valuing what others do and say, even though we might not agree, is (to my mind at least) the absolute beating heart of respect. It is where a plethora of other attributes and traits collide and intersect, including curiosity, humility, acceptance, empowerment, passion, justice and courage. Respect, whether you prefer the traditional definition or my own, is the place you land when all these other elements are on display and top of mind.

RESPECT IN THE WORKPLACE

It's interesting to note that respect is rarely mentioned in the modern workplace. Yet, in the survey of Members of the IML that presented more than 30 leadership attributes, and asked for them to be ranked in order of importance for sound leadership, respect ranked as the third most important attribute. It's clear that while respect isn't being discussed in leadership meetings, around the boardroom table, in HR culture sessions and informally among leaders, it is an important aspect of modern leadership.

Perhaps this apparent mismatch is due in part to the fact that, in a business sense, it can be hard to pinpoint the areas where we can improve on or influence respect. This is because respect is essentially a by-product of most people-based behaviours and principles. As an example, respect is typically gained by, among other things:

- Building trust
- Showing humility
- Leading with integrity and fairness
- Being authentic to who you are and allowing others to be authentic
- Decisiveness
- Setting purpose
- Consistency
- Clear and transparent communication
- Listening
- Encouraging and empowering others
- Having knowledge and experience
- Leading by example rather than direction alone.

Leaders who understand the value and the power of respect, and the impact that it can have on their leadership, recognise that the people they lead are individuals who have complex needs, which have to be fulfilled and nurtured. A team is not an entity in and of itself; it is a group of typically diverse and disparate individuals who share an office, a set of key performance indicators (KPIs), a corporate culture and a vision, mission and strategy. In order to enhance performance and create shared ownership of the team's goals, a leader must understand and take account of all of the idiosyncrasies and differences within that team.

Without respect, people will certainly follow systems and processes, but they are less likely to trust the overall direction of an organisation. In these situations, outcomes can be significantly limited. People may not be passionate about the vision of the business and its goals and so they may not walk confidently and productively in the paths we are treading.

Without respect, people may follow our words and do what we ask of them, but they are less likely to believe that we have the heart or integrity for what we are saying. In this sense, respect is key for leadership.

JOB SATISFACTION AND RESPECT

To further highlight the value of respect, the Society for Human Resource Management[1] in 2017 found that respect was viewed among employees as the greatest contributor to employee job satisfaction. This is shown in Figure 1.1 below.

Figure 1.1 – The greatest contributors to employee satisfaction

	Very satisfied	Very important
Respectful treatment of all employees at all levels	38%	65%
Compensation/pay, overall	26%	61%
Trust between employees and senior management	33%	61%
Job security	36%	58%
Opportunities to use your skills and abilities in your work	44%	56%

Note: n = 572-586. 'Not applicable' responses were excluded from this analysis. Data are sorted in descending order by the percentage of respondents who indicated 'very important'.
Source: *Employee Job Satisfaction and Engagement* (SHRM, 2017)

It is easy to see why this might be the case and why respect might be more important than we previously thought.

Respect requires a leader to go beyond simply understanding an individual's motivations, drivers and expectations. Good leaders become great leaders when they act and make changes based on their understanding of individual differences in their teams. Respect requires the leader to build interpersonal relationships with people that are grounded in a desire to understand, empathise and walk in other peoples' shoes. Great leaders learn to conduct themselves with integrity, honesty, humility and consistency with others regardless of their own beliefs. At its core, respect is about having due regard for our employees' beliefs. It's about putting other people first.

Case study: GM Holden – command-and-control versus respect-based leadership

Jamie Getgood

In the last 50 years we have seen an evolution of leadership styles; we have learnt more about personality types, neuroscience and the structure of the brain and the psychological drivers and impact of how we lead.

As a result of this research, management styles have evolved from being very process- and command-centred to empowering and people-focused.

There are, however, many industries and organisations still out there that are yet to master some of the finer strategies in people leadership. They have not seen the underlying principles of respect and how they can make a difference in an organisation.

I was fortunate enough to be involved in witnessing a real-life example of a command-and-control culture at GM Holden, which turned 180 degrees to one of respect for its workforce. I joined Holden in 2011, at a time of optimism as we had only 12 months earlier commenced building the Holden Cruze in Australia. This was an expansion of the range of vehicles built at our Elizabeth plant in South Australia, where we were already building over 100,000 Commodores (with that model's multiple variants and platforms).

As I inducted into the business, I was amazed at the great processes and technology used within the facility, but I could see from the very first week that there was a culture of dominance and autocratic leadership. I was surprised at the stringent and relentless focus on volumes and the aggression and passion that came when these metrics were not met. As a result, it came as no surprise that the business was not quite performing as it needed to be.

Concerned about how the employees were feeling, I would often walk the production lines within our General Assembly plant to see the culture at work. I would ask how people felt and what they saw as valuable to their life within the plant. One particular conversation with our union shop steward hit me hard when he remarked, *'What do you expect when our leaders don't even know us or respect us?'*. I remember standing there reflecting on my own negative interactions with one of our leaders and asked myself: *what are we doing?*

I suddenly realised that we had very little focus on our people who felt that we were not trustworthy, transparent, humble or even friendly. We didn't build relationships or communicate with them. We didn't trust them or show them any respect. As a result, our business results were not adequate and this was a reflection of our culture.

Resetting the people-first approach

Our results were fast becoming a concern, but I was extremely fortunate to have two executive directors in Ashley Winnett (People and Culture – Australia and New Zealand) and Richard Phillips (Manufacturing – ASEAN) who supported and helped drive the need to change our leadership approach.

I remember one afternoon when I was sitting with Richard and expressing my concerns about a negative and aggressive manager who didn't think people should be the main focus. Richard acknowledged that this style needed to change and we brainstormed what was needed to change our culture. Richard supported the concept and over the next 12 months we began to roll out a range of programs which included the following:

Walking in their shoes

This involved being more attentive to our people-related metrics, instead of how many cars or widgets we pushed out the door. We knew if we could build our engagement levels, improved results would follow. This program involved multiple approaches ranging from daily production walks, to getting to know our people, to physically getting on the production line and learning the experience of building cars and the challenges our employees faced. We also analysed our engagement surveys and developed employee-led workplace of choice teams to try to improve people metrics around trust, fairness, recognition, etc.

Improved communication

We committed to more consistent, reliable and transparent communication. We looked at our communication streams and found more effective, consistent and personal ways to communicate what was happening in our business. We used technology and phone applications so employees could receive the information directly on their phones. This new approach to communication removed the veil of secrecy in everything we did. Our employees and union representatives were always up to speed with what was happening.

The bigger picture

We had traditionally used a very capable manufacturing system that had always been pushed down on our employees. We decided to re-educate all our employees and empower them to drive the system themselves and be accountable for the outcomes in their areas. This also included explaining the 'why' behind everything we did so teams had a broader understanding of our processes and standards.

Playing your position

One of the reasons our culture had evolved into a command-and-control style leadership was because we had promoted technical specialists into leadership roles. This created two concerns. First, we had a generation of leaders who were leading but had little or no leadership training – they often did not have the behavioural capability to effectively lead people. Second, when a problem arose or a machine broke down, our top leaders would go out to try to fix the problem to 'help' speed up the repairs. This was not a good or appropriate use of their time, and it demotivated all those working at levels below them who were also trying to fix the problem. The solution to this problem was a training program we called 'playing your position', which ran through everyone's position and explained how each employee best served the organisation in the role they were employed to do.

Improved employee experience

We placed a strong emphasis on enhancing the employee experience by investing money and effort in reinvigorating the site and increasing levels of recognition as appropriate. This involved upgrading kitchen and bathroom facilities, repainting floors and walls, undertaking garden maintenance, etc. We also held social events, such as family days, charity events and classic car shows, which inspired and motivated employees within the workplace. Most of these activities continued despite the impending announcement of the closure of the plant.

These are just a handful of examples that highlight the people-first approach. It wasn't necessarily an easy journey; each step had its challenges and opposition and had to be carefully worked through to ensure our people remained the focus. Some leaders who weren't willing or able to be engaged in this approach were assisted in finding new opportunities – for some this meant leaving the organisation. It was impressive, though, to see some of our leaders who saw the benefits of our new-found direction become champions in leading their teams in this new way.

Respect through change and transition

The true test of whether you have generated respect and made a difference with your people is how they respond when you go through significant change or make decisions that potentially they don't agree with.

Holden had begun to make great inroads in transforming the organisation through the people-first leadership approach. The organisation was improving in multiple areas but was going through a new series of challenges that tested the respect, trust and commitment people had for their leaders and the organisation as a whole.

At the beginning of 2013, it was clear that the economic environment for automotive manufacturing in Australia was facing unprecedented challenges. The Australian dollar was high, there was a deterioration in the tariff system, free trade agreements and increased logistical costs were all taking their toll.

As a result of these external factors, it had become evident that we needed to do something significant to try to keep our manufacturing operation viable. We approached our workforce and union representatives to request they consider a variation to the Enterprise Agreement, which would see a reduction in a large number of conditions and pay rates. This was an attempt to reduce our labour-related costs and create a substantial business case for future car programs.

Traditionally, we had been very reluctant to share information with all employees, which had understandably resulted in poor levels of trust. This had often caused disputes with our people and unions, a reduction in productivity and a strong pushback on agreeing to variations in terms and conditions. However, now the workforce did trust that we were actually in the position we said we were in.

It was a telling moment in how far we had come as an organisation, and a reflection of the high quality of our leaders and employees. All areas of the new agreement were discussed with 100% transparency and were explained to all employees in detail, with due respect for how this news may impact their motivation and, more importantly, their families. Holden also gave a commitment that it would not continue with these reduced conditions in the event it had to close its doors.

Because of the level of respect and trust that had been built up, this agreement got voted up by 70% of the workforce, despite the conditions that were associated with it. This was a landmark achievement in this country, but this was not the end of the challenges.

No happy ending

Towards the end of 2013, the economic environment deteriorated to such an extent that it was no longer viable to build cars in Australia. Previously, we might have asked ourselves questions like:

- Do we cut our losses and close the plant immediately?
- Do we hold on to this knowledge as long as we can to shorten the time between the announcement and closure?
- Do we go to the media first to help save some brand reputation?

In the new environment, these types of questions were never even on the agenda. Instead, the leaders of the company made the announcement of the coming closure and a commitment to treat all employees with dignity and respect through the transition.

A clear, concise and transparent message went out to all employees, which honoured the pride in and reputation for our brand that the company had built over many years. The announcement included a four-year notice period that came with a commitment that Holden would do everything in its power to transition employees to the next phase of their journey.

To support this transition, Holden looked to a number of large closure programs from other multinationals all around the world to identify what was best for its employees. It invested $15 million in this four-phased approach, which was centred around a physical transition centre giving employees a place where they could go to get full support for both themselves and their families. The centre offered a range of services, including support with finances, health, small business training and job search support.

There was also an early release program, which allowed employees the opportunity to leave early with a reduced redundancy package should they be successful in obtaining a new role before the plant closed. This came with some risk for Holden as it still needed workers to continue building cars until the end of manufacturing period, but it gave employees the chance to leave with the best opportunity and the maximum amount of respect.

This program has been receiving praise from all over the world and has had transitional success rates of around 90% for those employees who left prior to closure.

On a personal level, I hoped as a leader that I had done all I could to support employees through these difficult times. To my surprise, I underestimated how much our employees appreciated the effort we had gone to throughout the transition. This has hit home to me a number of times when I have been out socially and bumped into ex-employees in the shopping centres and they have approached me with a genuine gratitude. Occasionally, I have received the odd hug thanking me for the respect our leaders showed them as they exited the organisation. That to me highlights the impact respect can have at the individual level.

The impact of respect on business results

Holden's change of leadership style and its direct approach in putting people first and building a culture of dignity and respect, led to tangible business results that not only improved the morale of the organisation but made a significant impact on the business scorecard and importantly on the bottom line.

After five years of work rebuilding the culture at Holden, and at the same time managing the closure of the plant, the organisation finished with the following business results in its last year of manufacturing cars in Australia:

- Absenteeism was under 4%.
- Holden received the safety award in 2016 as most valuable plant in GM International.
- We had five consecutive years as most significant cost improvement plant in GM International.
- In the final eight months of production, our plant was one of the best quality plants in the GM world.
- The majority of our engagement metrics – including trust, fairness, teamwork, recognition and commitment – rose by between 20% and 30% between 2011 and 2016.

It is clear from the GM Holden case study that building a people-first culture, and working on key aspects of this culture such as communication, transparency, fairness and trust can not only build and embed respect with your employees, but it can go a long way to improving the business results of your organisation.

THE 5 STEPS TO BUILDING RESPECT

1. Develop self-respect

One of the first principles to identify before you can obtain respect from others is the principle of self-respect.

> 'Respect for ourselves guides our morals, respect for others guides our manners.'
> —Laurence Sterne

I have learnt in my career that respecting others is clearly important, but having self-respect is a fundamental principle as you will only value others to the extent you are able to value yourself. Employees look up to their leaders subconsciously to develop a natural baseline as to what standards are acceptable; *what behaviours should I have and how valuable am I to the organisation?* How you respect yourself can make a difference to their viewpoint – and one of the most important aspects of this is the words you speak about yourself and others.

The words that we speak are powerful and can have a lasting impression on our minds, our hearts and the direction we will follow. Words can be used for encouragement or destruction and can be embedded into a person's heart before they can be taken back. Words have the potential to produce positive or negative consequences. They have the power to give life through encouragement and honesty or to crush and kill through lies and gossip.

I have seen this play out in my own home and it is no different in the workplace. If I am telling my children that they are little champions, they can do anything and they need to be positive, I am inspiring them to walk forward with purpose. If they, however, overhear me saying that I can't do something, I am useless and I should quit, it creates negative thoughts in their young minds that life is hard and if Dad can't do it, then what is the point? It is no different with our employees. How we respect and talk about ourselves sets a baseline for our employees who watch and are affected in similar ways.

2. Listen

Listening is another pillar of respect and is at the core of interpersonal relationships. By giving others your undivided attention you are showing them that you value what they have to say.

In the fast-paced, action-orientated world we work in, this is becoming a harder skill to acquire and is often not used well by leaders. In particular, busy leaders (and I am guilty of this) will often not have the patience to hear out a story. They will finish sentences in their head (or verbally) before the speaker has even got to the end. This is often where misunderstanding happens as sometimes the speaker was not thinking on the same wavelength as the listener and this can lead to conflict in extreme cases.

Be deliberate, patient (which can be hard for extroverts) and take the time to listen carefully to what is being said. Lean in and make good eye contact as your body language can transmit a message as much as your spoken words do. If you find it hard not to let your mind wander, try summarising what is being said in your mind.

Listening is not always easy for busy people and does require a conscious effort and lots of practice. It can also make a huge difference in showing respect for others.

3. Set the standard

It has been said that actions speak louder than words, and I have found that servant leadership can often play a part in setting a solid foundation and high standard. People will respond well and respect a leader who is willing to roll up their sleeves and help out when needed more than one who is always managing from their office. Respected leaders are those who consistently prove through their work ethic that they are reliable and trust-worthy on the inside and out.

Setting the standard isn't just about getting into the trenches though. The other part of setting the standard is being clear about the vision, goals and objectives that are required in the role. People respect clarity and direction and are much more efficient and engaged when they are working on the same path as the organisation.

It is equally important that employees feel engaged in the direction and that they can have some input into how the outcomes can be achieved. Involving employees in the goal-setting process can be powerful and can create empowered people who are thinking about how they can make a difference. When goals are achieved, these people take pride and ownership in themselves and the business, and this encourages them to go further and have higher expectations of achievement when the business provides its future steps and goals.

4. Be authentic

Authentic leaders are often the most respected as they are true to who they are and work with a strong sense of integrity, humility and trust. They are generally very aware of their own strengths, limitations, values and emotions and they do not act one way at work and another in private.

Authentic leaders make those around them feel as if they matter. It can be incredibly empowering to have a leader that you trust, and know that what they say is their word and that they will be loyal to you as they lead.

Authenticity comes from being transparent, consistent, open and available for the people around you. It requires honesty, humility and integrity and a leader with these qualities often inspires others by being a role model of the values that they stay true to.

5. Recognise and give feedback

As leaders, we are serving our people as much as they are serving our directive. Respect is often found when you ultimately know the people you serve and you regularly give them guidance, inspiration and support to enable more opportunities and help them grow. This can be achieved by leaders when they give feedback while also rewarding and recognising their people.

Your people may not always like feedback, especially if there are areas they need to improve in, but they will often still respect you knowing that you have been upfront about what the matter was and knowing your intent around growth. If you have made it a priority to know them and understand their core values, while their pride may be hurt, they will trust you and know that you wish to see them do well. Likewise, people appreciate being recognised and rewarded when they deserve to be and this can have a positive impact on their motivation and that of those around them.

THE MODERN COMPLEXITY OF RESPECT

Of course, all of this might seem to suggest that showing respect to your staff and to employees is relatively simple. The problem with providing a five-step guide to improving any personal attribute is that it tends to ignore the fact that people are complex and workplaces are made up of lots of people – and processes and systems and targets and KPIs. The reality is that suggesting that the panacea to showing respect in the workplace can be achieved in five steps is as simplistic as saying that you are five steps away from happiness! It is at best merely a starting point; a list of pointers that really only scratch the surface of the subject.

Respect is undeniably complex. This complexity is only increasing as the world – and the world of work (which, after all, is merely a microcosm of the wider world) – becomes ever more polarised, while it becomes ever more open. It's interesting that these two global trends seem to be in such conflict. Countries and workforces are becoming increasingly diverse, while public opinion about all aspects of diversity seems to be ever more polarised. We seem to be metaphorically pulling down walls, but leaders are appealing to millions who have notions of building physical walls. Barriers to trade and those that restrict the freedom of people to move and work across borders seem to be becoming mainstream policy directions, while political leaders argue forcibly for a reversal of these post-war trends.

These macro trends and developments make respect very much a fraught and complex thing. The typical workplace and team is incredibly diverse. A relatively small team of, say, 10 people might very easily be made up of any combination of female, male, people who identify as either or neither, people in same sex relationships, people with kids, people without kids, Christians, Jews, Muslims, Hindus, atheists, people with a physical or mental disability (or both) and people from quite literally any cultural background you can mention. In fact, it's safe to say that I have missed more 'categories' (and yes I detest that word) than I have listed. When all of these people – our workmates – arrive at work each morning, afternoon or evening, they do so in a social and political environment that is increasingly polarised and opinionated. Stereotypes abound, and the impact of these shouldn't be underestimated.

The best example I can give is from the UK following the Brexit vote in 2016, when Polish and other mainland European nationals living and working in London and other cities reported feeling an overwhelming sense of fear and uncertainty in the workplace.

Similar feelings were reported in Australia among the gay community during the same sex marriage debate and of course among the Muslim community each time a horrific terrorist attack takes place.

The seemingly constant attack on, and airing of, 'differences' in lifestyle choices, religious beliefs, cultural backgrounds, nationalities and other aspects of the rich tapestry of individuals' lives means that showing respect is increasingly portrayed as being unnecessary and, even worse, a sign of weakness.

RESPECT – IT'S ABOUT UNDERSTANDING, NOT AGREEING

Showing respect as a leader isn't about agreeing. It's simply not possible to agree with everyone about everything. Trying to do that is the quickest way to tie yourself up in knots and lose the respect of the team. It's also disingenuous.

When I joined CanTeen in 2002 as the Head of Fundraising and Marketing I met Carolyne, the Head of HR. We became and remain close friends. Carolyne is a committed and practising Christian, I'm a committed and practising atheist. We freely talked about – and laughed about – our very different life views and belief systems, and we frequently explained to each other why we had come to our own separate and diametrically different conclusions. That's life! As I once said during a conference keynote, 'if the workplace was full of middle-aged blokes from Manchester with a love of eighties music it would be a very dull place indeed!'. Difference and diversity is interesting, enriching and rewarding.

Respect is about understanding why people believe what they believe, do what they do and are who they are. Despite what we read and hear from a vocal section of today's media, and read on the more extreme reaches of the internet and social media sites, it's perfectly possible – and perfectly acceptable – to understand without agreeing. Showing respect as a leader is about accepting that you don't always need to be right, that there isn't necessarily only a right and wrong or just a black and white. Respect is about accepting and embracing the idea that other people's life experiences are different to yours and that that's OK.

As a leader, respect is about encouraging and embracing the view that difference and diversity bring strength to a team because they open the way to new thinking, new approaches and new ways of solving problems. Once this view is accepted it can be implemented in any number of ways within the workplace or team. For example, in recruitment, leaders should ensure that they do not fall into the trap of allowing personal bias to creep into the formal and informal recruitment process. In the same way, leaders need to guard against allowing their own views to cloud the way they deal with any number of issues and situations that arise each day in the workplace.

Making a statement – why IML released its Inclusion Statement

David Pich

'As the peak body for managers and leaders, we feel that it's important to recognise and value everybody – both in the workplace and in the broader community.

'We recognise the importance of allowing all people to feel comfortable and proud of who they are and we acknowledge

equally the contribution of people of all genders, sexes, sexualities, orientations, religions, cultures and races.'

In 2016, IML released its Inclusion Statement. This statement is now made – along with the Acknowledgement of Country – prior to every IML event. At its heart, the Inclusion Statement is a statement of respect. It captures quite nicely the essence of what the Institute believes lies at the heart of respect. Personally, I like to think of IML's Inclusion Statement as a challenge to today's leaders. Is this how you lead? Do you, as a leader, acknowledge the contribution of everyone in your team, regardless of gender, sexuality, religion, culture and race? Do you strive to create a company, a workplace and a team environment that allows all your people to feel comfortable and proud of who they are?

The Inclusion Statement says nothing about needing to agree with what your staff and colleagues believe and do. Inclusion isn't about agreeing, it's about accepting and understanding.

I like to think – naively perhaps – that when the Inclusion Statement is read out at IML events it has an impact, however small, on the people who hear it. Hopefully it makes them stop and think about a team member or colleague who is in a same sex relationship, or is from a different country or cultural background, or who has different religious beliefs – or no religious beliefs. Hopefully it makes that person curious to know a little more, to ask a few questions, to go a little deeper, to look beyond the news cycle and the headlines. You never know, the Inclusion Statement might even make people resolve to walk a mile in that person's shoes.

That mile is a real demonstration of true leadership respect.

Case study: IML and the same sex marriage debate

In 2017, the same sex marriage debate reached a crescendo around Australia as the Turnbull Government announced the first public plebiscite to be held nationally since the establishment of a republic plebiscite in 1999. The lead-up to the vote, as could probably have been predicted, became incredibly divisive and increasingly acrimonious as both sides of the argument, known as 'Yes' and 'No', stated their positions. During this time, numerous organisations, businesses, affiliations and societies made public statements in support of a Yes vote. Fewer organisations – mainly church bodies and religion-affiliated groups – and public and political figures made similarly public announcements in support of a No vote.

Partway through the 'campaign', I was approached by a number of IML staff with a suggestion that IML release a statement in support of a Yes vote.

The argument presented to me was that the Institute's recently published book, *Leadership Matters*, contained a chapter about the importance of inclusion in forming part of sound leadership practice. In addition, the Institute had just released its Inclusion Statement (see above) and this, the staff argued, was at its core a statement calling for respect of all people inside and outside the workplace. I found these arguments particularly compelling. It was also interesting to note that many other professional bodies and associations were releasing their own statements in support of a Yes vote.

I decided to ask the IML staff to prepare a discussion paper for the upcoming board meeting. While I supported the idea that the Institute should make a clear statement in support of a Yes vote, I felt that ultimately the board should be asked to vote on this. Since the board of IML is elected by and representative of the Membership this would make the statement much more powerful.

The Same Sex Marriage paper was tabled for discussion and a decision at the board meeting in July 2017. It's worth noting that the IML board comprises a broad cross-section of people from different sides of the political spectrum, of different religious and non-religious backgrounds, different industries and age groups. The board of IML is certainly diverse!

As it turned out, the board discussion of this particular agenda item didn't take too much time at all. All the board directors were absolutely in favour of the proposal. One director summed up the thinking of the group and of the IML staff with words along the lines of this being an issue of respect for others and an acknowledgement that equality and inclusion are key aspects of sound leadership. The Institute's support of the Yes vote wasn't about agreeing, it was about understanding that diversity, difference and inclusion are fundamental aspects of modern society and the modern workplace.

THE POWER OF THE SIMPLE THANK YOU. DOES GRATEFULNESS TRUMP MINDFULNESS?

My first job as a graduate fresh out of university was in the HR department at Cadbury Schweppes. I worked for the HR director, Graham Foulkes, and I have to admit that I found him quite scary and intimidating. With the benefit of that wonderful thing called hindsight I can see that this was entirely down to the fact that he drove a fancy car (a Jaguar XJ6) and he sat behind a big wooden desk in a big corner office. My feeling of intimidation was more to do with the fact that I wanted to have the car, the desk and the office. Graham wasn't remotely intimidating. He was simply a senior leader, and I was a fresh-faced graduate.

The very first project I worked on in that job involved documenting the various benefits that were offered to staff across the numerous Cadbury Schweppes manufacturing sites around the UK. The data from the project would be used to look at the viability of making these benefits more consistent. Over the next three months, I visited all the manufacturing sites and met the General Managers and HR managers at each to build my spreadsheet of benefits. At the end of the project I was invited up to Graham's beautiful office to present my findings.

I remember the long walk up to his office on the third floor of the building even today. I was absolutely petrified. The project itself had felt easy compared to this. I was presenting it to a proper leader – the first proper leader I'd ever known. He wasn't just a leader but a leader with a car I wanted, an office I wanted and a desk I wanted. In fact, he even had the job I wanted. I wanted to be the director of HR for Cadbury Schweppes. And because of that, I wanted Graham to be happy with what I'd done.

Anyway, long story short, he was. (Well, at least he said that he was). At the end of the presentation he said something else. It's something that has stuck with me for the past 25 years. He said: 'thank you'. He didn't just say it, he meant it. As I was getting up to leave his office, he asked me to sit back down and he actually said thank you. He explained why the project I had worked on was so important to him and to the company and why he was so pleased with the data I had gathered and what I had presented to him.

This story from my distant past has stuck with me and shaped me. I might not be the best leader all of the time, but I do definitely thank my team on a regular basis. I learnt this from Graham Foulkes. I remember how I felt when he said thank you to me. I felt great. The power contained in those two simple words is immense. As leaders we should never forget the power of gratitude. In a very real way, saying thank you is one of the easiest ways to show respect to your staff. It's not only easy; it's free! The payback of showing gratitude is also exponential.

There's something else about gratitude. It's something that is only just being realised and researched. It's long been known that an act of kindness, of a simple thank you, has a positive effect on the person who receives it, but what is now becoming clear is the impact of gratitude on the person giving it! In short, saying thank you is a double whammy – it's psychologically good for the giver and the receiver.

All the focus in recent years has been on the power of mindfulness. Think of all that money and energy that we have spent on yoga and meditating and adult colouring books, when actually the evidence points to gratefulness having a similar impact on us as mindfulness. As leaders, should we be quitting yoga and meditation and simply resolving to say thank you much more often to our teams? Perhaps not. But one thing is clear: gratefulness matters. Leaders need to understand that the foundation that respect is built on is found in two simple but incredibly powerful words: thank you. We should use these words much more often.

THE FINAL WORD ON RESPECT

Respect isn't something that is found in a box that you can purchase off the shelf. It is certainly not something you can 'do' overnight. Respect is earned and gained over time. We do not have to approve of someone's lifestyle, values or behaviours in order to show that we respect their humanity. The truth is that it is important to show respect whether the person deserves it or not.

Respectful behaviours are also not just for leaders or upper managers. All employees in an organisation can – and should – show respect for others. Whether you are actively listening to a workmate or empowering a team to be the best they can be, showing respect for others can make an enormous difference in the workplace. From creating a more engaged workforce to reducing conflict, respectful behaviours can boost morale and improve an organisation's productivity. Most importantly, a respectful environment promotes a culture where it becomes a pleasure to attend work each and every day.

Chapter 2

INTEGRITY

Michelle Gibbings

The thought manifests as the word.
The word manifests as the deed.
The deed develops into habit.
And habit hardens into character.
So, watch the thought and its ways with care,
And let it spring from love
Born out of concern for all beings…
As the shadow follows the body.
As we think so we become.

Buddha, in the Dhammapada

Author note

The issue of integrity is without doubt in the eye of the current leadership storm. When we read about a crisis of leadership it is almost always a reference to the integrity of those in leadership positions. In fact, in many ways good leadership has become synonymous with the idea of integrity.

It came as no real surprise therefore when Integrity was viewed by the Institute's Membership as the single most important attribute that good leaders must have to lead well. Integrity undoubtedly sits at the heart of effective leadership. As such, it was always going to be important to find someone to tackle this chapter who would be able to do it justice, someone who could speak with both authority and experience about the need for modern-day leaders to position themselves above reproach and to lead by example.

In Michelle Gibbings I'm delighted to say that we found the perfect author to tackle integrity.

Michelle is a longstanding Fellow of the Institute, a Chartered Manager, a regular keynote speaker and facilitator at IML's events, Masterclasses and Conferences and a respected author and media commentator on leadership in her own right. Her books Step Up *(2016) and* Career Leap *(2018) have cemented Michelle as an authority on management and leadership practice.*

I was thrilled when Michelle agreed to lend her expertise to this all-important leadership attribute, and I'm sure you will agree that her unique perspective on the importance of personal and professional integrity in leadership gives considerable food for thought for today's managers and leaders.

T HE SAYING GOES that it takes a lifetime to build a reputation and seconds to destroy it. The foundation of your reputation is integrity. A person with integrity lives their life according to moral and ethical principles, with honesty and trustfulness at its core.

At a practical level, your integrity is about what you say and do every day, the decisions you make and how you treat people.

People would bristle if they thought their integrity was being questioned, because it's a characteristic that's valued and not something they would want to lose. However, your integrity can become tarnished and eroded over time, if you're not careful.

In all quarters of society and around the globe we are seeing a downward shift in the public's trust of large institutions and established structures. The 2018 Edelman Trust Barometer, which measures the population of a country and their trust in four core pillars – government, business, non-government organisations and media – has revealed it's falling.

The 2017 Roy Morgan Image of Professions Survey found that of the 30 professions surveyed, 16 decreased their standing with regard to ethics and honesty, 12 increased and only two professions were unchanged. Health professionals (i.e. nurses, doctors and pharmacists) topped the list as most trusted, while politicians, journalists, advertising professionals and salespeople were at the bottom of the list.[1]

Of course, neither piece of research defines a person's individual level of integrity. It does, however, raise interesting questions about the impact that a working environment has on a person's integrity because of how they feel they need to behave and respond. At a time when the world is experiencing unprecedented levels of change and complexity we need leaders who guard their integrity and recognise its importance as a guiding principle for how they lead.

INTEGRITY IS EASILY CHALLENGED

Dan Ariely, a Professor of Psychology and Behavioural Economics, talks about the fact that everyone lies a little bit. *'We like to believe that a few bad apples spoil the virtuous bunch. But, research shows that everyone cheats a little – right up to the point where they lose their sense of integrity,'* he said.[2]

In research undertaken over a 10-year period, Dr Ariely and his colleagues used experiments and reviewed data from insurance claims to employment histories. What they found was that *'Everybody has the capacity to be dishonest, and almost everybody cheats – just by a little.'*

Ariely concedes that while there are a few exceptions, the vast majority are driven to cheating because they want to gain the benefit they will get from cheating – *'the money or the glory'.* Curiously though, they still want to regard themselves as *'honest, honourable people'.*

I find that explanation a little too depressing. I'd rather believe that not everyone is motivated by money and fame. That said, it is true that we are not always as ethical as we may think we are, and we can easily act without integrity. This is because we often make decisions reactively – letting emotion drive the decision-making process. As well, we are not always aware of the biases built into our decision-making process. The environment or culture in which we live and work plays a big part in the nature and scale of those biases. An organisational culture that tolerates or encourages behaviour that is 'dodgy' can see people behave in ways that are out of character. Behaviour that they wouldn't consider appropriate or ethical is adopted as they become 'culturalised' to the accepted way of behaving in that environment.

How are you showing up every day? Are you acting with integrity? Is your behaviour congruent with your stated values? If it's inconsistent, you will be sending mixed messages to people working with you and your integrity will be at risk.

In psychology, we use the terms 'espoused values' and 'values in use'. These terms were coined by Argyris and Schon back in 1974. Your espoused values are the values you talk about. For example, you might say you value honesty. Yet, if you are given an honest answer to a question such as *'Have I put on weight?'*, and the answer is *'Yes'*, you may not be happy with the response.

Your response is your values in use. Your values in use are the values that you use every day – at work, home and in all facets of life. To take two more examples, you might say you value the environment, but you don't recycle or do anything to improve the planet's health. You might say you value good leadership, and yet you exhibit poor leadership when dealing with direct reports you find hard to work with.

As those examples show, there is often a conflict and a gap between our espoused values and values in use.

History is littered with examples of people who were blind to the environment they worked in and the dangers this posed, and they didn't have the courage to protect their integrity. In the end, they became captured by the situation and their integrity was sold.

PROFIT AT ALL COSTS

Thousands of words have been written about Enron's culture and the consequential impact it had on the behaviour of people who worked there. In this culture, the executives and leaders at Enron were rewarded for their pursuit of profit regardless of the cost to consumers and society, and to behave otherwise was seen as unacceptable.[3] Their drive for profit at all cost filtered through the organisation, influencing the actions of many of the traders on the trading floor who bought and sold energy trades. The manipulation of energy during California's energy crisis (from 2000 to 2001) is well documented. Motivated by money, certain energy traders quite happily manipulated the system for the organisation's and ultimately their own personal gain (as they benefited via the company's bonus scheme).

PROFIT BEFORE SAFETY

The Ford Pinto was a very popular two-door, compact car that sold well in the United States in the 1970s. It had a major design flaw though – the fuel tank was in the back of the car, and if a car was rear-ended in an accident it could burst into flames. The company knew that the design of the car was causing deaths. It undertook a cost benefit analysis, which showed that it was cheaper to deal with the lawsuits from the deaths than to change the car's design. This was recorded in an internal memo, which highlighted the cost of reinforcing the car's rear-end ($121 million) versus the potential payout to victims ($50 million).[4] In the now infamous report, Ford often referred to *dead injured persons* as *'units'*.

ETHICS AND INTEGRITY TAKE A BACK SEAT

In more recent times in Australia, the Financial Services Royal Commission, established in late 2017, has seen a litany of examples in the banking and finance sectors of questionable behaviour – from unfair charging and product mis-selling, to charging fees for no service provided and continuing to charge fees to clients who had died.

I've seen people in organisations who considered themselves as ethical and having high integrity do things that other people would easily view as unethical. Often the unravelling of a person's integrity takes place little by little. A small cheat on a work expense claim, which goes unnoticed, gets larger over time.

At the other end of the spectrum, there are people who are conscious of their environment and who have the courage to remain centred and true to their principles. I've worked with leaders like this who operated with integrity and good intent. This created space and support for their team to be the best they could be.

When leaders act with integrity it permeates the culture of the organisation, enabling their teams to excel and thrive. It also means that they consider the impact of decisions not just in terms of what it means for them but what it means for customers, stakeholders, the environment and society as a whole.

PUTTING INTEGRITY AT THE CENTRE

Maintaining integrity encompasses two core attributes: having the courage to think and act, and being conscious of the environment or situation you are in.

Both attributes have a range (see Figure 2.1). You can think about courage in terms of being 'absent' at one end and 'present' at the other end, while your consciousness is either 'active' or 'passive'. How each attribute is activated will have consequences (either positive or negative) for your integrity.

Figure 2.1 – The core attributes of integrity

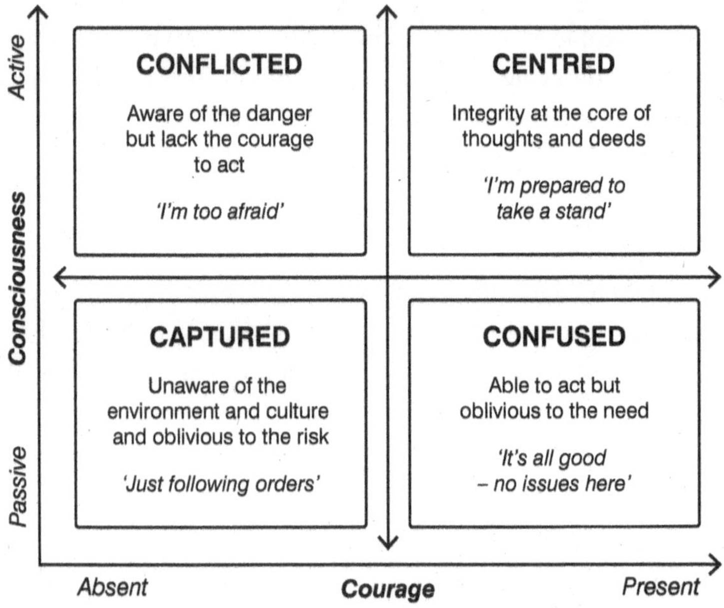

These are important dimensions to consider. If you have no courage and are completely unaware of environmental influences you are captured by what is going on around you, and you are very open to putting your integrity at risk. Such a person goes around oblivious to what is really going on. If you fall into this trap, you ultimately end up becoming complicit with bad behaviour when things go wrong. People in this category often say, *'I was just following orders'*. But, as history shows, following orders is never a good defence.

If you're conscious of what is going on but don't have the courage to act on it, you become conflicted. This is a terrible position to be in because the stress levels attached to being in this situation are extremely high. You know what is happening is wrong. You know there is something that should be done, but you don't have the courage to take action.

Social psychologist Leon Festinger[5] published his theory of cognitive dissonance in 1957. It explained the distressing mental state that arises when people find their beliefs are inconsistent with their actions. People in this state strive to bring the two into balance – and often it is their beliefs that will change, and so they end up being captured by the environment.

Without over-dramatising, reaching this point can be likened to the character Dr Faustus in Christopher Marlowe's late-16th century play of the same name. Dr Faustus sold his soul to the devil for power. It was not until he was about to die that he began to regret his actions and wanted to make amends. Sadly, by that time it was too late.

On the other hand, if courage is present but you have no aware-ness, you just end up being confused. You don't understand what is concerning people or why they are worried about what is happening. You have the ability to take action, but you don't know what needs to be done. You are oblivious to the situation and so ineffective in securing change.

You become centred when you have the balance of both courage and consciousness. This isn't always easy because maintaining integrity comes with risks and challenges. There are plenty of stories of people who have taken a stand in the face of enormous pressure and have faced backlash as a result. It often takes a huge personal toll. Interestingly, though, when they're asked about whether they would do it again invariably the answer is 'yes'.

In the 1980s, Jeffrey Wigand[6], a former Vice President of a United States-based tobacco company, went public with inside knowledge that tobacco companies had tried to conceal the dangers of smoking for years. His view was that he was clear on what and why he took a stand.

'The word whistle-blower suggests that you're a tattletale or that you're somehow disloyal,' he said. *'But I wasn't disloyal in the least bit. People were dying. I was loyal to a higher order of ethical responsibility.'*[7]

His action took a considerable toll; it impacted on his personal and family life and professional reputation.

When you know the right thing to do and you do nothing it eats away at your moral fibre. It's like a rotten apple. If the core is bad, it permeates throughout the whole.

At a broader level, if you're a leader your actions will be noticed and emulated. This plays out all the time in organisations. If the person leading the organisation is unethical, it filters through to how business gets done in that organisation. It's therefore critical to know what you need to do to stay true to yourself and to ensure your moral compass is pointed in the right direction.

I remember from an early age being told that if I was ever confused about a course of action and unsure about what was the right thing to do, I should use the newspaper test as a way of reflecting. This involves asking yourself: *'What would happen if my family or friends read about what I have done? How would I feel?'*

Knowing that your decision or action could become public often helps you make a good decision. Alternatively, ask yourself the question that Benjamin Franklin asked himself every day: *'What good shall I do today?'* and his evening question: *'What good have I done today?'.* What would your answers be?

STRENGTHENING YOUR INTEGRITY

If you want to be a more effective leader and stay true to your integrity, you need to start by accepting the fact that you're biased and, consequently, you can be blind to the obvious.

Psychologists Dan Simons and Christopher Chabris[8] conducted an experiment involving two teams. One team was wearing white shirts and the other team was wearing black shirts. The teams were filmed playing a ball game and this was played back to a group of people. They were instructed to count the number of times the ball was passed between the players wearing the white shirts and to ignore the team in black shirts. Halfway through the video a person wearing a gorilla suit appeared, thumped their chest and moved off screen. The gorilla is on the screen for just under 10 seconds. That's not a long time – but still long enough to think that people would notice.

When the researchers asked the people to say how many times the ball was thrown they got the number right. However, when they were asked about the gorilla approximately half the people watching the video had failed to see it. It's natural to wonder how that is even possible. It's possible because the instructions to count the number of times the ball is thrown and ignore the other team caused the brain to focus solely on that – to the exclusion of other things going on around it.

In many respects, this ability for the brain to focus, which is the brain's reticular activating system at work, is helpful. However, it can become unhelpful when the brain selectively ignores information that it doesn't think it needs to see. This is where bias creeps in.

Everyone has bias, much of which is subconscious. The danger is that this subconscious bias can get in the way of a good decision being made. When that happens you are no longer centred and this puts your integrity at risk.

Think of it like this. Your integrity is the compass that helps to guide you. However, if one of the elements in the compass is faulty, you will head in the wrong direction. If you don't know that the elements are faulty you can easily end up at the wrong destination, confused and lost.

Raising your consciousness, and establishing the courage to remain centred so your integrity continues to guide you in the right direction, involves three elements (see Figure 2.2).

Figure 2.2 – The strengthened integrity model

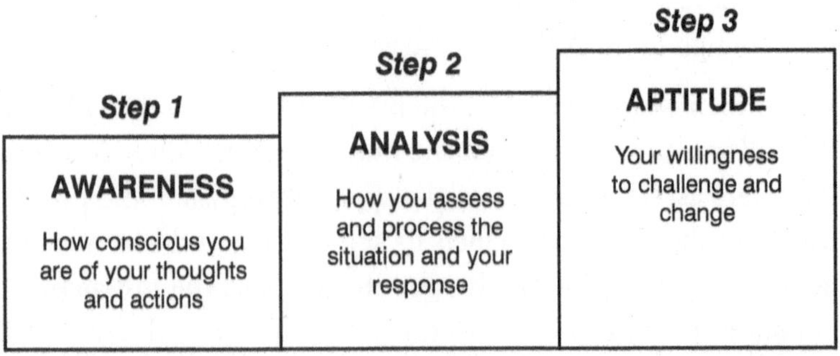

Step 1

AWARENESS

How conscious you are of your thoughts and actions

Step 2

ANALYSIS

How you assess and process the situation and your response

Step 3

APTITUDE

Your willingness to challenge and change

Awareness

It's important to understand the level of awareness you have about the decisions you are making, and the bias that may be influencing your decision-making. Consider:

- Are you aware of your bias preferences?
- Are you conscious of the limitations, assumptions or preconceived ideas that may be constraining how you think?
- Are you on the lookout for influencing factors that affect how you are processing information and making decisions?

Analysis

This is about how you analyse yourself and accept yourself for who you are, how you seek out information sources and ensure you are not stacking the decks in favour of your own world view. Scrutinise:

- Are you willing to take risks and back yourself, or are you easily swayed by the opinions of others?
- Do you have a clear purpose and understand what drives your actions?
- Are you seeking views from a range of diverse sources and considering the opinions from outliers, the silent minority and people who view the world differently to you?
- Are you devoting the right amount of time to the decision and including time for reflection?

Aptitude

Aptitude is your willingness to challenge your assumptions and preconceived ideas and the steps you are taking to account for different ideas and opinions when you make decisions. Examine:

- Are you willing to learn from your mistakes?
- Are you tired when making the decision, or too stressed and unable to focus?
- Are you taking care of yourself and putting yourself in the best position to make decisions?
- Are you putting in place clear steps and actions to filter out bias in your decision-making processes?
- Are you creating the optimal environment for healthy decision-making?

STEP ONE – ELEVATE YOUR AWARENESS

The first step in unplugging your bias is to elevate your awareness of the bias that exists.

Your brain loves bias. No doubt you think you're a highly rational being and that this rationality extends to how you make decisions. Unfortunately, that's not the case. Bias pervades decision-making because decisions aren't made on facts alone. They're made on hunches, feelings, past experiences and gut reactions.

You're not alone. Bias affects everyone. These biases are due to the way your brain makes decisions and to conditioning. Your brain is shaped by the experiences you have and consequently, over time, how you think and act can become fixed.

Every day – in all aspects of your life – you interpret the world through your lens of that past experience. Your past experience has taught you that certain things will happen in certain ways. It is these expectations that create assumptions. Your assumptions cause you to filter out information that doesn't fit with your world view, and instead you actively seek information that confirms what you think to be right or how things should be. Ultimately, these become blind spots, which are often at the root of differences of opinion and poor relationships.

Your brain at work

Your brain can be likened to a pattern-recognition machine and a massive filing system that likes to sort and categorise things. But your brain has limitations. The prefrontal cortex, which is the part of the brain that is actively engaged when you make decisions, has a limited amount of energy. Every time you make a decision energy is used, and so the brain finds ways to conserve energy. Similarly, your working memory has limited capacity, and so the brain has found ways to try to overcome this too.

Your brain is constantly and rapidly trying to make sense of the world and what is happening. To do that, and to ease the cognitive load this requires, it takes shortcuts. It compresses information and sorts it into patterns. By doing this it is making large tasks and complex issues easier to manage and, ultimately, remember (i.e. retrieve from the filing cabinet). Your brain is also very efficiently, but sometimes not all that helpfully, discarding information that doesn't fit with its world view.

While your brain is seeing, retrieving, sorting and making sense of information it is always trying to do it in the most energy-efficient way. It takes energy and time to store information in the brain, and it takes energy again to retrieve it. So, if the brain is trying to conserve energy it makes sense to try to find easier ways to do this. Without using predictive patterns or heuristics your brain would need to use dramatically more resources, putting a huge drain on the prefrontal cortex, to process what is happening and what you should do in response.

So your brain aims to take the path of least resistance as it works out what you need to do. This is where it gets dangerous because taking the path of least resistance means you will let expectations and assumptions drive how you think and act. Your bias will be out in full force – and your brain won't provide a warning signal.

Daniel Kahneman in his book *Thinking, Fast and Slow*[9] shared his years of research into this field. He explained the different modes of the brain's thought processes, labelling them System 1 and System 2. System 1 is the fast, instinctive, emotional and unconscious processing; while System 2 is slower, more deliberate, controlled and logical. It is the reliance on the automatic and instinctual part of the brain that predominantly leads to bias, as you place way too much confidence in your own judgement and opinions.

Cognitive bias

Kahneman explained the concept of 'anchoring'. This is a bias where people give disproportionate weight to the first piece of information they receive. This can be an impression, a number, a fact or a piece of data that impacts their subsequent thoughts and decisions. You will have heard the expression 'first impressions count'. You may not have realised the statement's significance extends beyond how people look. In fact, anchoring plays out when people buy houses and cars, or are in salary negotiations. The first offer made usually anchors the rest of the discussion.

Studies using the Implicit Association Test confirm the level of bias that exists in people. This test is used by social psychologists to measure implicit attitudes; that is, attitudes that a person may have that they may not be explicitly aware of. People taking the test are asked to make a split-second decision based on word and picture associations. In a particular example, participants are asked whether they have a positive or negative reaction to images of different types of people. At least 75% of people taking the test displayed bias. In this case, the bias was in favour of people who were young, rich and white. The study found that the mere desire to not be biased did not stop participants from being biased.[10]

What type of cognitive biases exist? At the latest count there are more than 100 scientifically proven brain-based biases. Those you will most commonly come across include:

- **Confirmation:** You ignore information that doesn't fit with your beliefs and actively look for evidence to support and back your position.

- **Anchoring:** As mentioned earlier, this is where you base decisions on the earliest piece of information you receive, ignoring later pieces of information that may be more relevant or correct.

- **In group:** Desire for acceptance and a need to be part of the 'in group' can cause you to conform and behave in a certain way due to the pressure of others.

- **Discounting:** The brain prefers rewards it can get now, and so you will sacrifice a bigger reward (that comes later) for a smaller reward (which is more immediate).

- **Mere exposure:** You prefer things which are familiar, and so being exposed to something over time can make you like something more than you did initially.

- **Status quo:** Preferring the familiar, you will actively defend and prefer the status quo and see it as better than alternatives.

- **Loss aversion:** The brain is wired to focus more on what you can lose than what you might gain.

These cognitive biases are strong because they are often interlinked and reinforcing. The danger is they impact decision-making processes and may combine in a way to produce unexpected and not necessarily positive outcomes.

I remember learning about the Bay of Pigs invasion when I was in high school. The invasion began when a CIA-financed and trained group of Cuban refugees landed in Cuba, with the objective of toppling Fidel Castro's communist-led government. The plan had been signed off by the then-United States President, John F. Kennedy, and it was a disaster. Studies of this event have shown that there were numerous issues that gave rise to the decision-making failures including: deference to authority, different opinions being dismissed and groupthink. Interestingly, many of the President's advisers had doubts about the plan, but they suspended their judgement and didn't say anything because they thought everything he did was going to succeed. They were blinded by their opinion of him.

In business, sunk cost traps are another perfect example. They're evident in organisations all the time. The organisation has made a decision to invest in a project and it will keep throwing money at it despite the evidence that shows it's time to shut it down. People don't like to admit they've made mistakes, and once an investment has been made it's often easier to keep going. The project team and sponsor can easily convince themselves to ignore information that shows them it's time to do something different.

It takes great courage to admit that an investment you've made is wrong. It also takes great insight and personal awareness to admit that there is a better way. Having worked on large-scale projects in big corporates I've seen this play out many times. Sometimes the dollars at stake were large and yet often reputational matters were of greater concern than the costs. The executive group that signed off on the expenditure was concerned about what it would look like if they stopped the project and naturally the project team was worried about keeping their jobs. The players involved often let their biases unconsciously invade their decision-making.

Having awareness that bias pervades decision-making is important, but it is only helpful if you do something about it.

STEP TWO – ANALYSE YOUR TRIGGERS AND ACTIONS

There are always different perspectives on what is right and wrong – particularly on issues that are ambiguous or complex. This means that good people can do things that can be perceived as dodgy, unfair or unethical from another person's perspective. It is not a black and white world! To remain centred, you need to objectively analyse what is going on around you. This includes accepting yourself and embracing the doubt that comes from knowing you don't have all the answers – and that's OK.

We can all build walls around ourselves, keeping our eyes closed to possibilities and new beginnings. We do this to protect ourselves. But, being in the dark and closed away from feedback, change and in some cases, reality, is not healthy. Having a growth mindset, and keeping your eyes and heart open is crucial if you are to thrive in today's environment.

Being authentic, comfortable to show vulnerability and naturally curious are important qualities if you want to be centred.

People who are uncomfortable with themselves and have low self-esteem are more easily persuaded by other people. We all have a desire for acceptance – to fit in and to be loved. When you feel unaccepted, you'll either try to conform or rebel. However, if you love yourself and who you are (even the flaws and imperfections), you are less worried about what people think of you.

Plus, if you know who you are, understand your trigger points and are happy with yourself, you are less likely to be enticed or led astray by others. This includes being led astray by the expectations imposed on you by others. Expectations can be helpful but, in many cases, they can be a constraint that holds you back from being the best version of you.

Knowing your true purpose

To break away from expectations you need to know yourself and what you want out of life. This isn't easy and we often struggle with what this means. It's impossible to stay centred when you don't know your core purpose. People who know their purpose are more easily able to overcome obstacles and to forge their unique path. They have the confidence to take charge and be in control of crucial personal decisions, which ultimately determines the course of their life.

There have been some brilliant books written about the steps you can take to identify your purpose and help assess the congruence with your work and life. Bill George's *True North*[11] is one example. It is worth reading as it takes you through a series of exercises you can do to achieve better alignment in your personal and professional life.

People find their purpose in different ways. For some people uncovering their purpose is about study, experimentation, building a business from scratch or raising a happy and healthy family. For other people it's about helping others, taking risks or venturing into the unknown.

Cheryl Strayed who wrote about her journey from 'lost to found' in the memoir *Wild* was one such person. She embarked on a three-month trek across the Pacific Crest Trail, covering more than 1,700 kilometres from Mexico to near the Canadian border. Relatively unprepared for the hike, she discovered much about herself and her resilience and fortitude through the journey.

In a different arena, Kathryn Bigelow broke the mould for women film-makers. Movies such as 'Hurt Locker' and 'Zero Dark Thirty' were not the type of films that women in the industry made. She ignored that. She said: *'If there's specific resistance to women making movies, I just choose to ignore that as an obstacle for two reasons: I can't change my gender, and I refuse to stop making movies.'*[12]

It's easy to be influenced by what is going on around you. If you don't like yourself and accept yourself, flaws and all, you're more open to the influence of others. This influence may not be good for you. It can negatively impact the choices you make as a leader.

What's even more dangerous is that you can close your eyes to what is really happening around you because of your desire to fit in and be liked. That heightens the chance of you being unaware of the potentially dangerous impact the working environment or culture is having on your ethical fibre.

The best option is to be constantly vigilant. This isn't easy. It's made harder by the fact that life is not clear-cut and there are always shades of grey, creating confusion and sometimes conflicted thoughts on the best approach to take.

Leaders are often told that they can't have doubt, and yet doubt can be good because it means you are questioning what you are doing. You are being purposeful, thoughtful and reflective. Doubt is unhelpful when it overwhelms you and stops you from progressing and making decisions.

Embracing yourself and using doubt as leverage is a step in the right direction. So too is taking the time to understand what is triggering the decision you are making.

Look for bias triggers

To help remove bias you need to be highly aware of your present state and your thinking patterns. This is meta-cognition. Thinking about how you think is only useful if you take the time to examine the bias that can creep into it, and what situational factors may give rise to it. This isn't easy. It takes immense courage to critically examine yourself. It is even harder to distinguish if there is a difference between what you are thinking and saying, and actually doing. That is, is there a difference between your espoused values and your values in use?

Look for triggers and ask yourself, are you likely to have bias in this situation due to:

- Past experience
- Background and upbringing
- Opinions of friends or people you respect
- Cultural conditioning
- Uncertainty and a desire to fit in.

After you've done that, consider how you can expand your field of view to take on board and consider different opinions and perspectives. This may include:

- Seeking information from people outside your normal circle of influence, to include different colleagues and people you don't yet know;
- Ensuring you are not overwhelmed by too much information or detail at the one time;
- Considering the outlier opinions and the voice of the silent minority;
- Spending time prioritising the information and using a clear process to sort, rank and select the possible outcomes;
- Critically considering what bias could be at play;
- Trying to remain curious and opened-minded throughout the decision-making process, and recognising that you don't know everything;
- Considering if you are letting your 'System 1' or 'System 2' brain drive the decision-making process;
- Taking the time to analyse the decision from multiple perspectives;
- Sleeping on the decision because looking at an issue the next morning will often provide a fresh perspective; or
- Reflecting on the decision to understand what you may do differently next time.

These are all building blocks that will help you build the aptitude for effective decision-making in which your integrity remains centred.

STEP THREE – CONSTRUCT YOUR APTITUDE TO TAKE ACTION

It's great to be aware and to understand what is driving you – your thought processes and actions – but it is meaningless if those insights don't translate into appropriate action.

Aptitude is your willingness to challenge your assumptions and preconceived ideas and to then take the necessary steps to act on that knowledge.

There are four primary practices to put in place:

1. Learning from mistakes
2. Picking your timing
3. Practising self-care
4. Structuring out the bias.

It is not enough to just do one of these practices. If you're eager to build the habit of better decision-making and ensure your integrity remains centred, you will want to put all of them to good use.

Practice One: Be ready to make learning-filled mistakes

No one is perfect, and everyone makes mistakes. Despite your best efforts, sometimes things will not go to plan. Consequently, not every decision you make will be a good one.

As Orlando A. Battista, a Canadian chemist and author, said: *'An error doesn't become a mistake until you refuse to correct it'.*

Being willing to step forward and admit mistakes can be hard, and yet it is integral to maintaining your integrity. If you are unwilling to admit your mistake and make amends, you are lying to yourself and those around you. When such behaviour is consistent and repeated it erodes your reputation, but even worse, you can start to believe your own self-talk and delusions.

Khaled Hosseini's novel, *The Kite Runner*, spells this out in beautiful prose. The story, which spans a number of decades, starts with two young boys from different sides of the racial divide in Afghanistan. A lie from one has a profound impact on the other boy's circumstances. But it was the boy who lied who subsequently lived with the guilt and regret. Over time, this ate away at him, propelling him to make amends.

Many business leaders failed at certain points in their career, and later went on to build very successful careers and businesses. Think Steve Jobs, Bill Gates, Richard Branson, Arianna Huffington, Vera Wang and Henry Ford.

It is not the mistake that defined them; rather it was what they did with the learning from that mistake, and their persistence to keep progressing. To be centred you need to know when you have made a mistake, accept it, recognise who has been impacted and be ready to make amends. This includes offering restitution and examining what happened and why, and therefore, being curious about the learnings you can derive from the experience.

To start, when an issue arises ask yourself:

- What happened?
- Why did it happen?
- Could I have prevented it from happening?
- What would I do differently next time?
- What would I not change?

Practice Two: Time decision-making to your advantage

As we become more tired through the day, we increasingly rely on our System 1 brain. When our brain is tired it falls into the trap of 'default thinking' – that is, deciding the way it has always decided and in the way that is easiest.

Consequently, it helps to treat the brain as a precious resource, where you do the most intensive, energy depleting activities first thing in the morning; scheduling less brain taxing things for later. This may mean you do complex problem-solving and report-writing first, while emails and social media activity can be left until later in the day.

What may surprise you is that 'busyness' can also interfere with ethical decision-making. When people feel pressed for time they can make decisions that normally they wouldn't have made.

In the early 1970s, John Darley and Daniel Batson (Princeton University) examined how time pressure affects behaviour. They invited students to participate in a series of experiments. In one of these experiments, the students were told to move from one building to another, with the testers varying the amount of 'urgency' in this message. To move between the buildings the students had to go past a person slumped on the floor and moaning. What the researchers found was that the more urgency in the message, the less likely it was for the person to stop and offer assistance. At the same time, many of those who didn't stop appeared agitated when they got to the next building. This was because they were conflicted in their desire to help and the instructions they had been given to get to the new building quickly.

People can fail to see what is going on around them when they are busy and preoccupied with timeliness.

Practice Three: Care for your heart, soul and body

Teachings from Eastern religions can provide useful food for thought, regardless of your religious beliefs. Putting aside the specific religious elements, these teachings offer useful insights into our humanity and what can be done to live a whole and just life.

Zen philosophy talks about the 'Four Limbs of Leadership'. These four limbs are: enlightenment and virtue, speech and action, humaneness and justice, etiquette and law.

In teachings, the writer uses the metaphor of a tree. *'Enlightenment and virtue are the root of the teaching; humaneness and justice are the branches of the teaching. With no root, it is impossible to stand; with no branches it is impossible to be complete'.*[13] What the writer is saying is we need to embrace our whole selves and be grounded to lead a full life.

Doing this requires a focus on looking after our whole selves – our physiology, neurology and psychology, and practising self-care where we look after our brain, gut and physical and mental health.

When you are tired, stressed, unwell or feeling under threat you are often more susceptible to making poor decisions and less well positioned to take rational and well thought through actions.

For example, if you feel stressed at work as the result of a boss's or colleague's actions there will be a whole raft of instinctive actions that arise. But, most importantly, when your limbic system (which includes your amygdala) is aroused it decreases the resources available to your prefrontal cortex; this is where the executive functions such as reasoning, analysis and problem-solving take place. When this happens you're more likely to make mistakes, have reduced working memory, be more pessimistic and less likely to solve complex problems. To top it all off, you're also more likely to react defensively, which isn't optimal for your integrity.

In times such as these you can veer off course, as you're less likely to consider the consequences of your actions and less able to see the other person's perspective.

This is where techniques such as mindfulness, meditation and reflection play an important role. They can calm your emotions and slow down your mind so you can then make a rational and well-reasoned decision. Similarly, staying fit and healthy enables you to better regulate your emotions and to find ways to expel unused frustrations and anger which, if left unresolved, can be physically and emotionally harmful.

Practice Four: Structure out the bias

There are structural approaches you can adopt to help remove bias. For example, using checklists helps you ensure that all bases are covered, while having clear assessment or decision-making criteria can assist to ensure that decisions made are more impartial and based on reason.

You can also 'blind' information so that you are not coloured by your bias. For example, some companies remove names and dates of birth from résumés so the person reviewing the CV only assesses it based on skills and experiences, and is not influenced by gender, ethnicity or age. Research has shown how successful this can be in improving the representation of women. For example, an orchestra that had the musicians play behind a screen during auditions saw the level of female representation in the orchestra increase from 5% to 40% over a number of years.[14]

Leaders need to put in place daily habits to help ensure they don't unwittingly put their integrity at risk, through a lack of information and understanding. These key habits could include:

- **Talking to people at all levels of the organisation.** Hierarchy can interfere with the information you receive as information can be filtered and sanitised before it hits your desk. People don't want to look bad, they want to paint the most optimistic picture of what is happening. Talking with people across and up and down the organisational hierarchy ensures you have a better handle on what is happening.

- **Being aware of gatekeepers, particularly if you are in a leadership role.** While your support staff will often be acting with good intent, if access to you is so heavily managed that it is impossible for people to see you, you will find it harder to have a realistic assessment of progress and issues.

- **Taking the time to walk the floor.** Casually walking around the office and stopping to have incidental conversations is an invaluable way of finding out what's going on. It's also a great way to build rapport and relationships with people.

- **Inviting differences of opinion.** When you are making decisions, make sure you involve people with different perspectives and backgrounds. This will help you engage in a broad level of analysis and debate before deciding. Out-of-the-box thinking often comes from unexpected quarters.

- **Constantly being alert to the weak signals.** Keep your eyes wide open to what is going on around you, and be naturally curious and questioning. If something doesn't feel right, it usually isn't. Trust your gut instinct and keep asking questions until you get to the heart of the matter.

- **Not silencing the dissenters.** It is often the person with the dissenting opinion, or the person who is asking the probing questions, who will help you see the issue from a different perspective. While this can be frustrating, it is usually helpful in the long run as you can take comfort from the fact that you have examined the issue from multiple angles.

In all of this, remember the words of the French philosopher Claude Levi Strauss: *'The wise doesn't give the right answers, he poses the right question'*.

THE FINAL WORD ON INTEGRITY

Your integrity as a leader and as a person is precious. Once it's tarnished it's hard to polish, and once it's gone it is very hard (sometimes impossible) to replace.

Guarding your integrity is crucial as a leader.

When you think of how you manage and elevate your integrity it is timely to recall the famous Native American story, which goes like this…

> *One evening, an old Cherokee tells his grandson that inside all people a battle goes on between two wolves. One wolf is negativity: anger, sadness, stress, contempt, disgust, fear, embarrassment, guilt, shame and hate. The other is positivity: joy, gratitude, serenity, hope, pride, amusement, inspiration, awe and love. The grandson thinks about this for a moment and then asks his grandfather, 'Which wolf wins?' The grandfather replies, 'The one you feed.'*

When you consider your integrity, the question to ask yourself is this: *'Which wolf are you feeding?'*

Chapter 3

EMOTIONAL INTELLIGENCE

Susanne Behrendt

No one cares how much you know,
until they know how much you care.

Theodore Roosevelt

Author note

A Chartered Accountant writing about the importance of emotional intelligence in ensuring that leaders lead well might well raise eyebrows. But, to be clear, mine were not remotely raised when Susanne Behrendt asked if she could write this chapter. Susanne is a true leader in every sense of the word and I didn't hesitate in entrusting this chapter and this leadership attribute to her more than capable hands.

Having led a professional association for Chartered Accountants (I was the Head of the Association of Chartered Certified Accountants Australia & New Zealand from 2014 to 2015) I can say with some authority that good leadership is alive and well in the accounting profession. Indeed, I really do think that it's a little too easy to slip into what I refer to within the Institute as 'discipline stereotyping'.

These days the 'professions' – including accounting, legal, medical and engineering, for example – are increasingly focused on management and leadership development. The result of this focus is leaders like Susanne, leaders who view leadership skill as being part and parcel of their profession and who focus on their own leadership development to the same extent as they focus on their technical development.

In many ways, this chapter – and the fact that it is expertly authored by a qualified accountant – represents the core of IML's mission and purpose. The Institute exists to facilitate the transition from the chaos of the accidental manager to the impact of the intentional leader.

Emotional intelligence – the ability to empathise with others and to adjust our own emotions and feelings to suit and adapt to a variety of situations – is what differentiates accidental managers from intentional leaders. EQ, as emotional intelligence is more commonly called, is often the 'magic dust' that is sprinkled on management to transform it into sound leadership.

I am delighted that Susanne is the one to sprinkle that magic dust in the chapter that follows.

AS A CHARTERED Accountant it might be surprising to learn that the very first non-financial business book I read was Daniel Goleman's seminal work and international bestseller, *Emotional Intelligence: Why it Can Matter More Than IQ*.[1] Modern thinking about leadership dictates – wrongly in my view – that accountants are not supposed to know about or be interested in leadership attributes like emotional intelligence. Yet, I was in my last year at high school and as a Psychology major I was fascinated by neuroscience generally, and specifically by the link (or otherwise!) between IQ and emotional intelligence.

Far from waning as my professional career diverged from my educational roots in psychology, my interest in the subject of emotional intelligence only increased. Perhaps this is down to the reality of my experiences in numerous workplaces over those years since university. On more than one occasion – many more, in fact – I have found myself thinking, '*Why on earth did this manager respond like that? Surely they could see the impact that their reaction was likely to have on the people around them!*'. Looking back over my career to date, I am convinced that it is my initial grounding in psychology and in the theory and practice of emotional intelligence that made *me* – an accountant – want to behave and lead people differently to the way that 'those' leaders led me and others.

In this chapter, we will explore the concept of emotional intelligence and why it plays such a crucial role in a leader's ability to lead well. Indeed, we will see that without this attribute it proves almost impossible to be a successful leader in the modern workplace.

EMOTIONAL INTELLIGENCE – THE ELUSIVE LEADERSHIP ATTRIBUTE

The first time I was alerted to the importance of emotional intelligence in the workplace and to its pivotal position in the management toolkit was in my very first role as a young manager with a small team of direct reports. I had 'inherited' a team member whose performance did not meet expectations for the professional role that he was in. Being new to the team and to management, I listened to what my predecessor and other managers in the organisation had to say and I spent some time observing what was actually going on. The team member seemed committed and was clearly trying hard, but something was holding him back. He appeared frightened and insecure at times. I chatted at length to the HR manager who suggested that we should set up a meeting to allow the team member the chance to discuss his concerns (or fears) about his role with us and for me to outline a proposed performance management process.

The HR manager opened the meeting with my staff member, saying *'We are here today to talk about your performance. We are not talking about terminating your employment, yet. But let me be very honest – this is one of the options at the end of this process.'*

As you can well imagine, it was all downhill from there! The meeting did not go well at all and the natural response from my already fearful team member was for him to shut down and retreat further into himself. The meeting became more of a performance improvement session that was led by HR, than an opportunity for us to explore what might be going on for my member of staff. At the best of times, after that opening, it would have been a tough journey back towards constructive conversation. In this case, it simply didn't happen. The meeting ended with me still in the dark about what was going on for the staff member and him clearly even more distressed. He left the team soon after.

We probably all have multiple examples like this where we are taken aback by the way that professional people judge – or misjudge – situations and interact with us and others in a way that seems to fly in the face of their professionalism. Despite their extensive experience, myriad professional qualifications – often including management degrees and an MBA from a top-notch business school – it seems clear that a decent grounding in emotional intelligence and how to conduct empathetic conversations with colleagues, staff, clients, customers, patients and family members is severely lacking. This is often especially true when it comes to conveying difficult messages about personal matters, performance issues, redundancies, illnesses and the like. What appears to be very much management 101 is in reality the Holy Grail of management practice. Emotional intelligence would appear on the surface to be relatively simple and really quite obvious, and yet it remains perhaps one of the most elusive leadership attributes. Indeed, it's hard to disagree with Daniel Goleman's assertion that:

> '(These days) CEOs are hired for their intellect and business expertise – and fired for a lack of emotional intelligence.'[2]

DEFINING EMOTIONAL INTELLIGENCE

Emotional intelligence (EI) is commonly referred to as EQ or emotional quotient. These terms entered the management and leadership conversation in the mid-1980s when two American psychologists, John D. Mayer and Peter Salovey, began to study the way that leaders reacted to certain workplace situations. In the 1990s Daniel Goleman, another American psychologist, built on their work and succeeded in making the topic far more accessible. Today, emotional intelligence is one of the most widely referenced terms in leadership theory and practice. It is certainly prominent among the selection criteria for the vast majority of management and leadership roles and it would be very unusual for an interview panel tasked with filling a junior, middle or senior manager role not to address examples where a candidate has displayed strong EQ. It's safe to say that EQ is the flavour of the month in management and leadership and it's very likely to stay that way for a long time. EQ matters; it's arguably the leadership attribute that sets a leader apart and causes a good leader to be great.

The concept of emotional intelligence is widely understood as:

'recognising one's own emotions, and acting on them in a reflective and critical manner. A person with high EI is generally expected to be very self-aware, to have strong self-control, to reflect on his or her own feelings and behaviour and to be able to empathise well with other people. While very aware of their feelings, those with high EI resist any impulsive, 'spur of the moment' reactions to emotions, and instead, base their actions on a reflective consideration of their feelings, the situation, and possible responses and their consequences.'[3]

Research by Dr Benjamin Palmer at Australia's Swinburne University saw the development of the Genos Emotional Intelligence Model[4] (see Figure 3.1). This defined a set of six workplace competencies that are both observable and measurable. Together they are now considered to be a strong indicator of how emotionally intelligent someone is. In addition, Palmer's model links emotional intelligence with what he refers to as positive or negative productive states. The model outlines the core elements of emotional intelligence and the personal state of each for the individual.

Figure 3.1 – Genos Emotional Intelligence Model

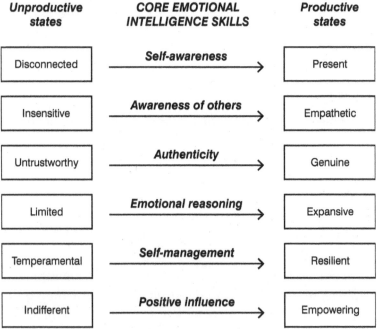

Unproductive states	CORE EMOTIONAL INTELLIGENCE SKILLS	Productive states
Disconnected	Self-awareness →	Present
Insensitive	Awareness of others →	Empathetic
Untrustworthy	Authenticity →	Genuine
Limited	Emotional reasoning →	Expansive
Temperamental	Self-management →	Resilient
Indifferent	Positive influence →	Empowering

Source: https://www.genosinternational.com/workplace-behaviour/

In the Genos Emotional Intelligence model, these six categories are defined as:

- **Self-awareness** – Being *aware of the way you feel* and *the impact your feelings can have* on decisions, behaviour and performance. People who are emotionally self-aware are conscious of the role their feelings can play in these areas and are better equipped to manage this influence effectively.

- **Awareness of others** – *Perceiving, understanding and acknowledging the way others feel.* This skill helps us identify the things that make people feel valued, listened to, cared for, consulted and understood. It also helps us demonstrate empathy, anticipate responses or reactions, and adjust our behaviour so that it fits well with others.

- **Authenticity** – *Openly and effectively expressing oneself,* honouring commitments and encouraging this behaviour in others. It involves honestly expressing specific feelings at work, such as happiness and frustration, providing feedback to colleagues about the way you feel, and sharing emotions at the right time, to the right degree and to the right people.

- **Emotional reasoning** – *Using the information in feelings* (from oneself and others) *when decision-making.* It involves considering your own and others' feelings when making decisions, combining the information in feelings with facts and technical information, and communicating this decision-making process to others. Feelings and emotions contain important information. For example, the level of commitment colleagues demonstrate often provides insight into whether a decision is going to be supported; the emotional appeal of products and services often provides insight into selling and marketing messages. When this type of emotional information is combined with facts and technical information, people make expansive, creative and well thought-through decisions.

- **Self-management** – *Managing one's own mood and emotions, time and behaviour,* and continuously improving oneself. The modern workplace is generally one of high demands and pressure, and this can create negative emotions and outcomes. Our mood can be very infectious and can therefore be a powerful force in the workplace; productive or unproductive. This skill helps people be resilient and manage high work demands and stress rather than being temperamental at work.

- **Positive influence** – *Positively influencing the way others feel* through problem-solving, feedback, recognising and supporting others' work. It involves creating a positive working environment for others, helping others find effective ways of responding to upsetting events and effectively helping people resolve issues that are affecting their performance. This skill helps people create a productive environment for others. Positive influence equips you with the capacity to encourage colleagues to cooperate and work effectively together.

Reproduced with kind permission from Dr Benjamin R. Palmer, BAppSci (Hons), PhD, Chief Executive Officer, Genos International, www.genosinternational.com

CMI's EI Indicator – a quick check!

For an initial indication of where you and your team members sit on the scale of emotionally intelligent or 'productive' behaviours, you can take this quick quiz that has been developed by the

Chartered Management Institute (CMI)[5] in the UK. It serves as a good tool to start the conversation with your team members about EQ. The quiz is designed as the first step in an ongoing process and as a precursor to more indepth personal development focusing on emotional intelligence.

Mark the most appropriate column: 1 = never, 2 = rarely, 3 = sometimes, 4 = usually, 5 = always.	1	2	3	4	5
Self-awareness					
You are aware of how you are perceived by others					
You are aware that your moods can affect others for better or worse					
You are confident of your abilities and feel that most people respect you					
Emotional resilience					
You are determined to see things through to completion					
You are comfortable when you have to overrule others' firmly held views					
You are easily depressed if things go wrong					
Motivation					
You always look for new challenges and to exceed existing targets					
You always encourage your staff to do the same					
You find it difficult to exercise self-discipline					
Empathy					
You find it hard to be a good listener					
You take into account other people's concerns					
You sense what other people are feeling without being told					

	1	2	3	4	5
Social skills					
You feel uneasy talking to large groups					
You are comfortable when meeting and dealing with new people					
You always try to get people to work together, not against each other					
SCORE					

To arrive at your score, multiply the number of times that you ticked each column by the number at the top of the column, then add up the outcome of all the columns.

Your score out of a maximum 75:

Please note, this test has not been empirically validated and is intended only to give an illustration of a few of the many characteristics that can make up the overall concept of emotional intelligence and how they can be assessed to provide indicators for development.

LEARNING EMOTIONAL INTELLIGENCE

Some of the latest research suggests that we are born with a certain level of intelligence or mental ability and that this develops and changes during adolescence.[6] According to the CMI Emotional Intelligence Checklist[7] many researchers today believe that emotional intelligence follows a similar pattern and that we are essentially born with a certain EQ capacity. While there is little empirical evidence for such a thing as an 'inborn' EQ, there is widespread agreement that emotional intelligence involves the ability to be empathetic and to understand and take into consideration the feelings of the people around us when making decisions. The foundations for such cognitive abilities are typically developed early in life, during a person's childhood, and the absence of a nurturing and stimulating environment during those early years is often associated with a lack of social skills in the teenage years and adulthood.

A study conducted by Marsland and Likavec in 2003[8] found that maternal scores of emotional intelligence, as well as the quality of mother–child interactions, were highly correlated with preschool children's display of empathy and prosocial peer relations. That is, the mothers' EI was a high predictor of their children's social competence. Other studies that compared EI scores in adolescent and university-aged students did not find significant age-determined trends in the development of EI.[9]

Across the three major models of emotional intelligence, views differ on the degree to which EI can be developed through training:

	Ability models	Trait models	Competency models
Definition of EI	A set of mental abilities related to emotions and the processing of emotional information	A set of interrelated socio-emotional traits, e.g. assertiveness, that determine intelligent behaviour	A set of emotional competencies defined as learned capabilities that contribute to performance and leadership

	Ability models	Trait models	Competency models
Ability to develop EI	EI is seen as a relatively stable aptitude; only emotional knowledge can be taught and acquired	Model focuses on the measurement and predictive ability of EI, rather than how it can be changed over time	EI can be developed and learned like any other cognitive skill
Key researchers	*Mayer and Salovey*	*Bar-On*	*Goleman*

Source: Spielberger, C. *Encyclopedia of Applied Psychology*, 2004

When it comes to emotional intelligence in management and leadership my own view is that change is possible. From my personal experience, as well as from the more cognitive behavioural models of psychology, I feel that the competency model is the model that offers the best guide.

The competency model holds that if you follow some key principles that are required to change a pattern of behaviour, there is a good chance that you will succeed. These principles are:

1. **Know exactly what you would like to improve** – start with a 360-degree EQ assessment and focus on a few areas for improvement at a time.

2. **Motivate yourself to make a change** – create a 'vision board', set achievable goals and celebrate your progress.

3. **Find yourself a mentor or coach** – studies show that coaching programs work better than self-study for EI and

one of the most effective coaching techniques in this area seems to be cognitive behavioural therapy.

4. **Identify role models** – this will set an example that you can strive for.

5. **Be patient** – humans are animals of habit and behaviours change only through repetition.

Curiosity at the heart of emotional intelligence

Gunnar Habitz CMgr FIML

Pulitzer Prize winner Thomas L. Friedman promoted the terms curiosity quotient (CQ) and passion quotient (PQ), arguing that they are even more important than emotional intelligence: CQ + PQ > EQ.

While curiosity has long been accepted as a useful learning tool in this ever-changing world, it is now widely thought to also develop emotional intelligence. In my own leadership journey, I was promoted from an individual contributor to an accidental manager working across 29 countries in central and eastern Europe. This was also a transition from a business development role within a stable market to a sales management position in an emerging region.

The European VP of Sales was my 'dotted-line' manager and he saw the region like one country and expected me to handle the nuances between the different cultures, demographics and market developments in the same way. In this newly created position, I had to earn the trust of the country teams first. I soon realised there were vast differences between mature and emerging businesses, and open sharing and hiding knowledge practices. Each country negotiated differently and then of course there were the language barriers.

I decided to take my motivation from Simon Sinek's book and *Start With Why*. My wife was born in Czech Republic and I already knew one Slavic language and understood the culture. My new role offered me the great opportunity to live in Prague for longer than just over the odd weekend, it offered me the full working experience. My 'why' was the adventure of embracing this region professionally and personally.

Right from the start I have built my personal brand around a double interest: people and places. For some months each year, I worked out of Prague instead of my Swiss home town of Zürich to learn the daily life in the region. This helped me to break the ice when approaching my new team members, partners and customers.

While I had been used to mostly using a coaching style in my former role managing more mature ex-colleagues, I had to now adopt more mentoring activities to help my new sales team step up. I was curious about their career progression during different technology lifecycles, which made them regard me as a help and not a controlling factor sent from European headquarters.

Using my visionary and participative leadership styles, I was able to create a culture of eagerness about the customer segment and to enable trust between the team members. Soon I obtained the local knowledge of an expat about Moscow, Warsaw and Budapest rather than just the knowledge of an infrequent business visitor who only knows airports, offices and hotels. My developed interest resulted in me writing a number of published articles about those cities covering theatre, gastronomy and history.

This applied curiosity into the people and their environment was at the base of my understanding of the challenges of my team members, in their professional and personal lives. Adding CQ to IQ and EQ was the driving factor in achieving these results. Another driver has been the right combination of constant learning about my new marketplace and remembering my earlier experiences. Many international managers do the reverse, attempting to apply their old life experiences to the new place without fully embracing the new people and geography.

I am a true believer in active networking. Whenever I got the chance, I brought the team together for face-to-face sales training, small events and presentations with customers. I always engineered the seating arrangements to make sure the team sat next to someone from another region who spoke a different language. They soon started to share stories and learn from each other. Facilitating curiosity makes it possible to unlock empathy for the other person using a hook – such as a warm introduction, handling a common account in different countries or simply exchanging best practice during a break in meetings.

After a successful first year, we experienced a downturn. A more typical manager might have then switched to a directive approach to push for higher sales numbers without satisfying a real purpose. But I chose to continue to use CQ and EQ, and connected more closely with my peers in other regions – in particular in the larger countries like the UK, France and Germany – to learn about their market situation and what really kept them awake at night. Later, they were keen to learn what worked well in my region when their economy experienced a downturn and our European business was booming.

My international experience gave me a genuine interest in the team members and I developed a passion for their environment. This allowed me to place myself in their position to 'feel' their situation and to adopt the own emotions. Honest curiosity is the base for constant learning about the world around us and it also encourages us to act more entrepreneurially.

When my wife and I moved to Australia in 2016, we actually didn't know anybody except two friends who lived in Melbourne. In the beginning, I went to several networking events and started an Advanced Diploma of Leadership and Management at AIM. Instead of telling everybody my story, I used my curiosity again to learn about the Australian people and marketplace. As an engineer I always want to know how everything works.

Moving 'down under' has been a life experience that has brought unexpected personal growth. Curiosity has enabled me to build strong personal and business connections, consolidate my personal brand and apply my passion in helping others: that is leadership by serving.

EMOTIONAL INTELLIGENCE IN THE WORKPLACE

Since the 1980s, when the concept of emotional intelligence was first discussed, numerous studies and researchers have sought to investigate the link between how people feel in the workplace and how they perform in their roles. There is overwhelming evidence that points to a strong correlation between emotionally intelligent leadership, high performance and higher employee engagement.

Emotionally intelligent leadership is also considered to have an impact outside of the walls of an office, with customer loyalty and strong supplier relations being attributed to it, often resulting in better overall organisational performance.

IML's landmark 21st century leadership research finds that EQ is a key leadership attribute

During 2018 and early 2019 IML conducted a research project to consider the primary needs of employers in developing their employees' leadership skills, and the impact of universities in meeting these needs. The research involved over 780 respondents, including discussion groups, indepth interviews and an online survey with current and recent business degree students and employers.

Key skills associated with IML's leadership competency framework were specifically referenced and measured during the data collection phase. This allowed IML's research team to understand what leadership competencies were in high demand, what skills were lacking, and what graduates entering the workforce required to improve employability.

- Throughout the data gathering stage it became clear that the 'soft skills' or 'human skills' usually came to the fore. There was the need for greater emotional intelligence and resilience in the workplace. This was particularly evident where employers were asked in the survey to rate the strengths of their employees with business-related degrees whom they had hired and managed.

- Ratings of the competencies varied (see Figure 3.2). Employers considered that their employees were 'somewhat' or 'very' strong in relation to decision-making and problem-solving skills (74%), developing and maintaining professional networks (73%) and managing time and priorities (also 73%). In contrast, employees were relatively poorer in the area of fostering emotional intelligence and resilience, with 35% of surveyed employers categorising their employees as 'weak' or 'somewhat weak'. This remains a concerning statistic for IML's research team.

Figure 3.2 – Strength of self-management competencies of employees

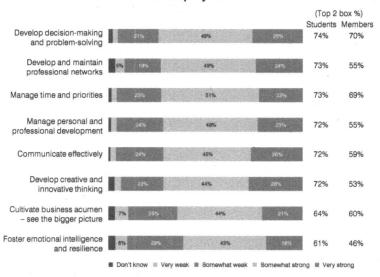

Base: Employers, unweighted, n=535. Members, unweighted, n=68.
Note: Labels less than 5% have been removed for clarity.
Source: B16. Thinking generally about employees that you hire/manage with business-related degrees in Australia, in your experience how strong or weak are their following competencies related to self-management?

Key data from employers also highlighted the importance of emotional intelligence for new and current managers. It showed that 39% of employers regarded emotional intelligence as a desired skill for new managers, but this increased significantly to 53% for current managers. This provided clear evidence that emotional intelligence and resilience was not only a key competency for existing managers and leaders, but also an important skill that should be understood and developed for aspiring and new managers.

The research examined the university sector through the eyes of their students – this included the university contribution to the development of soft skills. Specifically, at least 8 in 10 students indicated that their university 'very much' or 'somewhat' contributed to them gaining a range of self-management competencies (see Figure 3.3).

Figure 3.3 – University contribution to self-management competencies

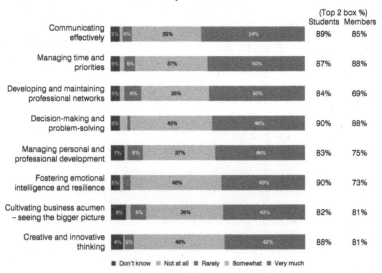

Base: Students, unweighted, n=127. Members, unweighted, n=48.
Note: Labels less than 5% removed for clarity.
Source: C15. To what extent is your university helping/did your university help you to gain the following self-management competencies?

Interestingly, universities were strongest in terms of helping students with communicating effectively (54% of students said their university helped 'very much'), managing time and priorities (50%) and developing and maintaining professional networks (50%). In contrast, universities were weaker in relation to helping students foster emotional intelligence and resilience, with 52% of respondents replying 'somewhat', 'rarely' or 'not at all'.

This highlights the need for universities to do more for their students in the development of emotional intelligence skills. Indeed, 84% of employers surveyed believe emotional intelligence and other 'soft skills' should be integrated into all degree-level subjects to both improve employability and to improve students' success as employees.

EI AND LEADERSHIP STYLES

In the *Harvard Business Review* article *Leadership that gets results*,[10] Daniel Goleman described a study of emotional intelligence and leadership styles.

Taking into consideration the findings of nearly 4,000 executives who participated in this study, Goleman suggests that leaders are most successful adopting a combination of six different leadership styles that use and emphasise various aspects of his Competency Model of Emotional Intelligence.

The study suggests that these six emotionally intelligent leadership styles are not mutually exclusive and that we should apply the most suitable style depending on the situations and the type of teams and projects that we encounter in the workplace.

Leadership style	Characteristic features	EI components most used
Coercive	Demands immediate compliance	Is self-motivated, initiates change and is driven to succeed
Authoritative	Mobilises teams towards achieving a common goal	Initiates change and is empathic
Affiliative	Builds emotional bonds and harmony	Is empathic and builds relationships; has strong communication skills
Democratic	Aims for consensus through involvement in decision-making	Is good at communicating, listening and negotiating
Pacesetting	Expects excellence and self-motivation	Uses initiative, sets high standards of performance and is driven to succeed
Coaching	Develops people's skills for the future	Listens well, communicates effectively and motivates others

It is interesting that the standard leadership question in an interview situation is often, 'What is your leadership style?'. This study suggests that the answer to this question is far more complex than the typical answer ('my leadership style is consultative'). In fact, Daniel Goleman concluded that no manager should ever just consider adopting only one of the six styles. He maintains that with practice, leaders can learn to identify the most appropriate style to use in a certain circumstance and that the goal should be that leaders focus on mastering the ability to switch between these styles to create the best outcomes for different individuals and different situations rather than simply following one personal 'signature' style.

In future interviews, perhaps a better question would be, 'Tell me about your different leadership styles and the situations in which you deploy these.'

EI AND RECRUITMENT

Traditionally, recruitment and talent attraction relied on skills-based assessments and using past experience as a predictor of future performance. However, many organisations have started to integrate measures of emotional intelligence into their recruitment process. This is mostly done in the form of psychometric assessments and role-play based simulations. Cary Cherniss describes the following study in 'The Business Case for Emotional Intelligence': [11]

'For 515 senior executives analysed by the search firm Egon Zehnder International, those who were primarily strong in emotional intelligence were more likely to succeed than those who were strongest in either relevant previous experience or IQ. In other words, emotional intelligence was a better predictor of success than either relevant previous experience or high IQ. More specifically, the executive was high in emotional intelligence in 74 percent of the successes and only in 24 percent of the failures. The study included executives in Latin America, Germany, and Japan, and the results were almost identical in all three cultures.'

Generally, three different methods can be used for measuring emotional intelligence both on an individual as well as a team level:

1. **Self-assessment** – an individual's rating of their own emotional intelligence.

2. **External assessment** (180 or 360-degree feedback) – a group's rating of an individual's emotional intelligence.

3. **Ability/performance assessment** – the ability/performance in a particular circumstance is assessed for signs of emotional intelligence.

"Yes, I think I have good people skills.
What kind of idiot question is that?"

© Glasbergen www.glasbergen.com

For HR professionals, a wide range of tests and scales for emotional intelligence are readily available these days, some of which include the following:

Abilities-based tests

Measure emotional ability similarly to cognitive ability (IQ)

- Mayer-Salovey-Caruso Emotional Intelligence Test (MSCEIT)
  http://www.eiconsortium.org/measures/msceit.html

Behaviour-based tests

Measure how frequently a person demonstrates emotionally intelligent behaviours and actions

- Genos Emotional Intelligence Inventory (Genos EI)
  https://www.genosinternational.com/recruitment/

Competency-based tests

Measure a person's emotional intelligence competencies against expected levels

- Emotional and Social Competence Inventory (ESCI)
  http://www.eiconsortium.org/measures/eci_360.html
- Group Emotional Competence (GEC) inventory
  http://www.geipartners.com/

Trait-based tests

Measure emotional intelligence as a trait like personality or disposition

- BarOn Emotional Quotient Inventory (BarOn EQ-i)
  http://www.reuvenbaron.org/wp/
- Trait Emotional Intelligence Questionnaire (TEIQue)
  http://psychometriclab.com/obtaining-the-teique/

Source: http://eiconsortium.org/measures/measures.html

Note: The information above provides an overview of some of the EI tests publicly available at the time this book was written. The above list is neither exhaustive nor endorsed by the Institute of Managers and Leaders.

As with investment products, the principle that 'past performance is no guarantee of future performance' also applies to recruitment tests. Using them as a single source of predicting an applicant's success in the organisation is likely to result in disappointment. However, scores derived from a reliable and valid test of EI have successfully been used in shortlisting and comparing applicants together with determining the individual's motivation, cultural fit and technical skills that can be explored better in structured interviews or case studies.

EQ and recruitment assessments

When building and developing teams, understanding your people is critical to optimal performance and success. In recruitment, the more insight you have on your candidates, the more likely you are to make the right selection decision. Psychometric assessments give you real insight into whether a candidate is likely to succeed and help your business grow. More specifically, resumes, interviews and reference checks only tell part of the story – the part a candidate wants you to hear. Psychometric assessments reveal a much larger picture. Using scientifically proven methods, they can accurately predict how a candidate is likely to perform, whether they are likely to be engaged, and their potential commitment to the business. Assessments allow you to collect large amounts of data in a very short amount of time. They significantly speed up shortlisting and decision-making processes, while increasing the quality of hire. When they are part of a robust recruitment process, psychometric assessments can be the missing piece that ensures you hire the best people. For more information regarding the types of personal attributes and abilities that can be assessed during the recruitment process, please refer to https://managersandleaders.com.au/recruitment/.

Data driven decisions are also important in employee development, in understanding the strengths and areas for improvement for each team member. These tools provide a valid means of predicting performance together with a tangible profile of your existing team. Furthermore, self-awareness and personal insight are the first steps in adjusting behaviour and powerful tools in professional development. Psychometric assessments use established frameworks to analyse your behaviour and preferences and natural attributes, and they provide you with targeted suggestions for future development.

For example, the Revelian Behavioural Profile – Development (RBP-D) is underpinned by the premise that people who understand themselves well in terms of their strengths and weaknesses are more effective in professional and social situations. The assessment is based on the well-respected DiSC model of behaviour developed by William Marsten in 1924. It analyses a person's behavioural preferences in the context of the four factors of DiSC:

1. **Dominance** – how they deal with problems and challenges
2. **Influencing** – how they interact with and influence other people
3. **Steadiness** – their preferred pace and approach to work
4. **Compliance** – how they deal with rules and procedures set by other people.

The report offers deep insight into a person's unique natural and adapted behavioural preferences – how they prefer to act when they're most relaxed as opposed to how they've adapted their behaviour to meet current demands. It provides detailed information around their strengths, motivators, ideal work environment and development areas, and is an excellent way to pinpoint specific behaviours to target and improve.

Another useful tool for self-awareness and development is the Emotional Intelligence Test – Development (MSCEIT-D), which analyses a person's EI abilities. As we've learned in this chapter,

EI is a critical skill in many professional and social environments, and the MSCEIT-D is designed to actually test EI as an ability, rather than asking people to rate themselves. In this way, it gives you a very objective and accurate assessment of a person's level of EI across several different areas: perceiving emotions (how accurately the person can correctly identify emotions), facilitating thought (how well the person can use emotions to solve problems and make more effective decisions), understanding emotions (correctly defining and labelling emotions and reasoning with them effectively) and managing emotions (understanding how different actions influence emotions and using emotions in a rational and considered way). The report gives an overview of the amount of development required in each area and steps the recipient can take to improve their effectiveness.

EI AND SUCCESS IN SALES

How would you feel entering a car sales yard looking for a new family-sized SUV and the salesperson shows you a two-seater sports car? Agreed, it probably has a bigger engine, accelerates faster, the beige leather interior looks very sleek and on top of all that it comes at a 10% discount (only if you buy it today, though). Did the salesperson listen to you? Did they understand and correctly analyse your needs and concerns? Were they focused on the product (and potentially the higher sales commission) or on solving your problem?

Over the last decades, the idea of emotionally intelligent sales tactics has entered the arena of sales professionals' training and development. Psychometric tests are often used at the beginning of such training or at the recruitment stage. These tests aim to determine the degree of 'sales call reluctance' and other behaviours associated with the initiation of social contacts, a key requirement for a successful sale. In their article 'Sales call reluctance among Americans, Australians and New Zealanders', published in 2001, Bernstein, Dudley and Goodson[12] concluded that:

'EI may be a better predictor of sales success than:

1. *How much experience people have in sales.*
2. *How bright sales people are (IQ).*
3. *The behavioural preferences and styles they have (personality).*
4. *Other popular measures used in the recruitment of sales people […]'.*

Case study: Enhancing sales performance through emotional intelligence development

Sue Jennings and Dr Benjamin Palmer (2007)

Background

In a study involving Sanofi-Aventis sales representatives in Australia in 2006, Dr Ben Palmer and Sue Jennings compared the outcomes of pre- and post-training EI assessments for sales representatives and sales managers (to whom the sales representatives reported) before and after they participated in a six-month EI development program.

Approach

The six-month program included:

- 360-degree feedback assessment focusing on EI to benchmark EI at the start of the training.

- Individual action plans developed based on the outcome of the 360-degree feedback.
- Small group coaching sessions linked to each of Genos' six emotional intelligence skills.
- Behavioural rehearsal activities.
- 360-degree feedback re-assessments.
- Individual action plans developed based on continuous future development and self-coaching.

The EI development program for the sales representatives and managers varied slightly with the managers being involved in the representatives' coaching and learning how to lead with emotional intelligence, while the representatives' program focused on how to develop emotionally intelligent sales skills.

Findings

Change in the mean EI of the group that participated the EI development program over six months:

- Sales representatives: +18%.
- Sales managers: +7% (the lower increase compared to the sales representatives was explained by a related study that showed that most individuals in leadership positions already possess well-developed emotional intelligence competencies).
- The mean EI of the control group that was not offered the EI development program stayed more or less the same between assessments, decreasing by 4%.
- Importantly, sales revenue generated by the sales representatives that participated in the development program improved by 13% while the revenue of the control group remained constant. The 13% improvement in revenue meant the program returned $6 for every $1 Sanofi invested in the program.

Conclusion

Sue Jennings and Dr Ben Palmer concluded that 'the emotional intelligence of sales professionals can be improved through the emotional intelligence training and development programs, and that such development produces significant return on investment'.

A further qualitative analysis of the program undertaken as part of the study suggested that the program improved:

1. The sales managers' leadership capability.
2. The relationships between the sales managers and the sales representatives.
3. Participants' job satisfaction.

Reproduced with kind permission from Dr Benjamin R Palmer, BAppSci (Hons), PhD, Chief Executive Officer, Genos International, www.genosinternational.com

EI AND PERFORMANCE MANAGEMENT

One of the more challenging aspects of being a manager and leader is often to performance-manage staff who do not meet the same output and behaviour standards as their peers. Interestingly, the majority of performance management issues seem to stem from employees' lack of self-awareness, which is one of the six key competencies that Genos and Goleman identified in their models of emotional intelligence.

We constantly provide feedback to the people around us in our workplace, both formally and informally and intentionally and unintentionally. Employees with a sound level of emotional intelligence seem to pick up on it and take it on board without issues ever becoming a cause for concern and escalating to require formal performance management. Employees who lack self-awareness – the conscious knowledge of your own personality and emotions and how these two are perceived in interactions with others – often seem to resist feedback and either react defensively or pretend to take it on the surface but then don't act on it.

From my experience, there are three aspects of emotional intelligence involved when it comes to performance appraisals and management (see Figure 3.4).

Figure 3.4 – Three aspects of performance management and appraisals

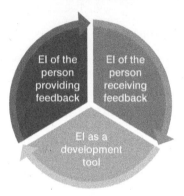

1. **The EI of the person providing the feedback** – The example that I gave in the opening paragraphs of this chapter described clearly what not to do in a performance management conversation. The simple prospect of an upcoming performance appraisal fills many employees with doubt and worries and promotes defensiveness. If the person providing the feedback is unaware of these emotions and the way his or her style triggers or – worse – exacerbates these feelings for the employee, the performance review process can be ineffective and straining on the relationship between manager and employee. It is therefore important that managers and leaders are trained in emotional intelligence and how to remove employees' feelings of anxiety and uncertainty from the performance review process.

2. **The EI of the person receiving the feedback** – Where employees enter the performance appraisal process with an open and positive mind rather than the thought *this conversation is going to be terrible and I will hear all the bad things that I have done,* the feedback process has much more productive outcomes. Emotionally intelligent employees are able to take a view that performance appraisals are an opportunity to reflect on the previous months and their achievements. It is also an opportunity for them to develop plans for their role in the organisation and for personal development with their manager. Emotionally intelligent employees are able to bounce back and process negative feedback much better due to having skills of resilience and self-motivation. The person providing the feedback needs to understand the degree of emotional intelligence that their employee is equipped with and lead the performance conversation accordingly.

3. **Use of EI as a development tool** – Where performance issues have arisen, and the employee seems to be unable to take the feedback on board due to the lack of competencies such as self-awareness, undergoing an EI assessment and discussing the results rather than the actual performance issue can be helpful. The results of the EI assessment often come as a surprise to the employee and can get them to focus and commit to changing behaviours. There are often underlying reasons for poor performance or social interaction with their peers. When individual development plans are combined with EI skills training and supported by coaching to reinforce new behaviours, research has shown that positive results are achieved.

EI AND NEGOTIATIONS

On my way to work on the train I recently saw someone reading the book *Never split the difference – Negotiating as if your life depended on it*[13] by Chris Voss, a former international hostage negotiator for the FBI. No doubt this person has way more experience in negotiating in highly political and life-threatening situations under extreme time pressure than I have (to be completely honest – my track record in this field is zero), and the author is probably also extremely well trained in world-leading psychological and negotiation tactics (again – my track record here is zero). However, from my experience in real everyday life, negotiating with emotional intelligence is often contrary to negotiating as if your life depends on it.

Looking at the most common scenarios for negotiations, both in a work or business environment as well as in our personal lives, I like to distinguish between:

1. **Transactional negotiations** – very infrequent or one-off purchases in a location and with a party that you are highly unlikely to meet again or depend on in the future. *Examples:* Buying a washing machine for your daughter who has moved to a different city to start university or purchasing a new company car; and

2. **Relational negotiations** – one-off or repeat purchases in a location close to your home or business and with a party that you are likely to deal with again in the future and that you have or would like to establish a relationship with. *Examples:* Entering into an IT services agreement for your organisation or agreeing a holiday destination with your family.

While transactional negotiations – as their name suggests – can and should focus on the transaction and the outcome for yourself or your organisation (but never forget ethics!), relational negotiations should be co-operative and focused around problem-solving (for all parties). Relational negotiations benefit from transparency, from both parties sharing as much information as possible to understand each other's interests and problems.

Being able to apply the principles of emotional intelligence to negotiations, by:

- understanding your own as well as the other party's feelings and motivations;
- considering these feelings and motivations in the process of the negotiation;
- being courteous and realistic; and
- taking an interest in the future of the relationship

is the most powerful form of negotiation tactics.

Giving the other party what they want and helping them understand what you want and how they can give it to you will create a win–win situation. In the short term, relationships might survive transactional negotiations, which are often characterised by strong power-imbalance (think of the family-owned farms delivering their produce to large supermarket chains that dictate prices and conditions). However, only relationships that generate positive and sustainable outcomes for both sides will grow and survive in the long term. At the risk of sounding like a relationship counsellor, long-term relationships, both in the business and personal world, offer greater security and many benefits from the indepth knowledge about each other that the partners accumulate over time.

The Human Moment

In an article published in the *Harvard Business Review* in 1999, Edward Hallowell talked about 'The Human Moment at Work'. In times of ever-increasing use of technology and anonymity in the office and our lives, personal interaction with people around us can make a significant difference. People prefer the use of email over making a phone call or having a face-to-face conversation with their family and colleagues. But just think back to that joyful moment when you last received a handwritten card for your birthday or Christmas and how special you felt! When did you last sit at the dinner table with your family and have an engaging conversation? The typical sight in restaurants these days is people sitting next to each other, while each individual is immersed in messages and games on their mobile phones.

The strategic use of the 'human moment' both in the workplace and our personal space is a very practical application of emotional intelligence and can help reduce the ambiguity of electronic communication and develop confidence and trust. It also reduces the worry, mental fatigue and disconnection associated with the excessive use of electronics – try it out!

THE LAST WORD ON EMOTIONAL INTELLIGENCE

One idea about being an emotionally intelligent leader that particularly appeals to me, and a connection that I would not necessarily have made before starting to research this chapter, is the concept that leading with emotional intelligence can actually result in a better work–life balance and mental health – for both our teams and ourselves. Why is this?

Employee engagement surveys show over and over again that leadership (or the lack thereof) is a major cause of employee disengagement and stress. Disengagement and stress, in turn, have been proven to have a negative correlation with productivity and staff retention rates. Prolonged and high levels of stress lead to underperformance and ill health, both in the workplace and at home. In the US it is reported that the main causes underlying up to 40% of staff turnover and up to 80% of work-related injuries are related to stress.

EI development programs teach stress coping strategies (benefiting ourselves) and workplace competencies such as:

- Self-awareness
- Awareness of others
- Authenticity
- Emotional reasoning
- Self-management
- Positive influence.

Leaders who display high levels of these skills reduce stress for their teams, foster healthy and positive relationships and acknowledge the importance of taking breaks from work, both during the day and in the form of annual leave. These leaders are also associated with displaying and promoting physical exercise and healthy eating habits, which in turn can help prevent severe chronic stress (often referred to as 'burnout syndrome') and other mental illnesses.

Chapter 4

ABILITY TO INSPIRE

Sam Bell

Before you are a leader, success is all about
growing yourself. When you become a leader,
success is all about growing others.

Jack Welch

Author note

The elusive ability to inspire those we are fortunate enough to lead is perhaps the Holy Grail of successful leadership.

It really needs no introduction. I will leave it to the expert, Sam Bell, one of the Institute's very own inspirational leaders to explain why it matters and how you can add a dash of inspiration to the way that you lead!

I NSPIRATION IS POSSIBLY one of the most overused words of the modern world. Books, social media feeds, blogs and memes are full of inspirational – and inspirational sounding – quotes and soundbites. Even theories of leadership have shifted from the more traditional systems of rewards and punishment, control and scrutiny to those that focus on innovation, individual character and the courage of convictions.[1]

There can be little doubt that one of the most important elements of a leader's role is finding the balance between being transactional and being transformational – and transformational leadership is based on possessing the ability to inspire others!

TRANSACTIONAL, TRANSFORMATIONAL AND SITUATIONAL LEADERSHIP

While transactional leadership focuses on the role of supervision, organisation and group performances, with the status quo and day-to-day progress toward goals being the primary concern, transformational leadership seeks to enhance the motivation and engagement of people by directing their behaviour towards a shared vision. The transactional approach features positive and negative reinforcement, whereas transformational leadership stresses motivation and inspiration.

A transactional leader is someone who focuses on managing the day-to-day tasks and processes within the work team. This is an important role because the daily tasks and processes are what keep an organisation operating. Transactional leaders tend to focus on workflow, organising resources and on performance and compliance with rules.

A transformational leader by contrast is someone who focuses on challenging people and teams to change, to grow, to develop and – very often – to challenge the status quo. These leaders strive to engage their teams with a shared vision, and they use their energy and enthusiasm to inspire their people to follow them. It is often the case that transformational leaders attract 'followers' rather than staff or employees.

Of course, most modern-day leadership analysis suggests that in order to inspire team members you need to strike a healthy balance between the transactional and the transformational. This thinking created the concept of *situational leadership* which describes a situation where a leader possesses the ability to change their approach depending on what is needed to get the best outcome.

Situational leadership means that while sometimes a leader will need to focus heavily on workflow and performance in order to 'get the job done', at other times the same leader will need to focus on *how* the team members are feeling and will ensure that they are emotionally supported to keep morale and productivity at the optimal level.

A variety of external factors have contributed to this evolution in thinking about leadership style. The pace of technological change has meant leaders have to be responsive and adaptable to lead their teams through change. There's heightened uncertainty in global terms with the threats of terrorism and insecurity in peace time. People need to be reassured that their leaders are putting their wellbeing first. The changing workforce questions an organisation's loyalty to them and is searching for meaning in the workplace.

MOTIVATION OR INSPIRATION

The shift from transactional leadership to transformational leadership and then to situational leadership has brought more focus on the importance of motivation and inspiration as key leadership skills.

It has been argued that of the two, inspiration – the ability to inspire – is the more important leadership skill.

Marissa Levin distinguishes motivation as being *pushed* to accomplish a task; that is, being motivated by a result. Whereas inspiration is about being *pulled* towards something that stirs your heart, mind or spirit: *'the most inspirational leaders ignite a spark within their employees and followers that move them to action. They don't require motivation to act because they've been inspired'*[2] – by a person, event or circumstance.

It is reasonable for global management teams to fixate about employee engagement, but ultimately leadership, in a world of infinite choices – where so much power to build value sits with the employees – is about inspiration.[3]

Inspired employees exhibit three key characteristics. They are:

1. **Authentically dedicated** – proud of their organisation for how it acts in the world and therefore they are self-driven.
2. **Deeply accountable** – seizing authority, meeting obligations.
3. **Fully responsible**.

In addition, inspired staff tend to be extraordinarily productive. The HOW Report, 'A Global Empirical Analysis of How Governance, Culture and Leadership Impact Performance', characterises inspiration as 27% more predictive of performance than engagement, which is contingent and transactional, hence only as strong as the organisation's short-term performance and the employee's career trajectory.[4]

According to the report, eventually that transaction, driven by rewards, perks and other incentives, will expire, while inspiration – fuelled internally by deeply held beliefs and the connection between those beliefs and work – is enduring and profound.

It found that the key behaviours of inspirational senior leaders were that they:

- Shared stories that exemplified how the organisation's values came to life.
- Held themselves accountable to standards of conduct in line with the organisation's values.
- Explained the role of values in making key decisions.
- Publicly admitted their own mistakes.
- Honoured commitments made to others.
- Sought feedback to strengthen their leadership and increase their own impact.
- Regularly connected with employees in meaningful ways.
- Held themselves responsible for the team's successes and failures.

In summary, the ability to inspire others comes from a set of beliefs and behaviours that start with the leader themselves. An ability to inspire is at its heart an internal process that others see and, by definition, find to be inspiring!

THE ROLE OF EMOTIONAL INTELLIGENCE IN INSPIRATIONAL LEADERSHIP

As we learned in the previous chapter, over the last 30 years, the importance of emotional intelligence (EI or EQ) in a leadership role has grown exponentially. Indeed, EQ is now widely recognised as a critical aspect of inspirational leadership.

There's a close link between emotionally intelligent leadership and employee performance and satisfaction. There are five pillars to emotional intelligence:

1. **Self-awareness** – leaders with high emotional awareness can develop skills that allow them to respond effectively to situations that come up in the workplace.

2. **Self-regulation** – control of the leader's potentially disruptive emotions and impulses and ability to adapt to changing situations.

3. **Social awareness** – being able to connect with others and be likeable; having organisational awareness.

4. **Empathy (social skills)** – relating to others and building strong sustainable leadership.

5. **Motivation** – improving to achieve, commitment to organisational values, visions, mission and goals, acting on opportunities and displaying optimism and resilience.

Higher EQ correlates with better work performance and inspirational leadership far more reliably than higher IQ. Moreover, it can be learned through the implementation of professional leadership assessment tools such as MSCEIT and Genos emotional intelligence testing.

THE NEUROSCIENCE OF INSPIRATIONAL LEADERSHIP – I AND ME VERSUS US AND WE

According to the social identity theory of leadership, effective leaders are able to conceptualise a group-oriented vision of the future that those they lead identify with. This is often achieved by creating a sense of purpose among employees and emphasising the critical element of future collective success.

One very simple technique is to replace the use of 'I' and 'me' with the more inclusive use of 'we' and 'us'. One memorable example of this was Barack Obama's 2008 presidential election campaign that was built on the simple – and yet inspired – phrase, 'Yes we can'.

A recent study that analysed the Australian election speeches of prime ministerial candidates during the last 43 elections suggested further support for this theory, noting that leaders who used the 'we' or 'us' reference (rather than 'I' or 'me') won the election approximately 80% of the time.[5]

A recent brain imaging study supports this premise. It found there was a strong in-group bias towards messages being more inspirational when they were believed to be emanating from an in-group leader, as indicated through fMRI imaging results (see Figure 4.1). More activation in brain areas involved in information processing was noted when observing inspirational messages as opposed to non-inspirational messages from an in-group leader (brain A); however, no increase was seen by comparison when the messages were from out-group leaders (brain B).[6]

Hence, it is crucial that leaders create a vision and a group identity that employees can identify with in order to be viewed as inspirational. This involves focusing on creating the best outcome for the whole group rather than just the best outcome for the leader.

Figure 4.1 – fMRI imaging results from inspirational and non inspirational messages

A.   B.

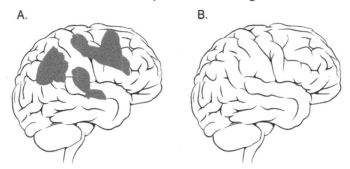

Source: Molenberghs et al., (2015) 'The neuroscience of inspirational leadership: The importance of collective-oriented language and shared group membership', *Journal of Management*

INSPIRATIONAL LEADERSHIP WITHIN ORGANISATIONS

There are many organisations that have achieved outstanding results under the direction of inspirational business leaders. Jim Collins, author of *Good to Great*, explored leadership within modern companies and completed a research project that used empirical evidence to help identify factors that enabled some companies to become significantly more successful than their competitors given the same market conditions.

These success factors included having inspiring people in an organisation and creating a culture of discipline and momentum through consistency and focus.

From their research, Collins and his team came up with the concept of Level 5 Leadership.

The five levels are:

- **Level 1: Highly capable individual.** At this level, you make high-quality contributions with your work. You possess useful levels of knowledge; and you have the talent and skills needed to do a good job.

- **Level 2: Contributing team member.** At Level 2, you use your knowledge and skills to help your team succeed. You work effectively, productively and successfully with other people in your group.

- **Level 3: Competent manager.** Here, you're able to organise a group effectively to achieve specific goals and objectives.

- **Level 4: Effective leader.** Level 4 is the category that most top leaders fall into. Here, you're able to galvanise a department or organisation to meet performance objectives and achieve a vision.

- **Level 5: Great leader.** At Level 5, you have all of the abilities needed for the other four levels, plus you have the unique blend of humility and will that is required for true greatness.

Reprinted by permission of *Harvard Business Review*. From 'Level 5 Leadership: The Triumph of Humility and Fierce Resolve' by Jim Collins, January 2001. Copyright © 2001 by the Harvard Business School Publishing Corporation; all rights reserved.

The findings show that the leaders from 'Great Companies' had more 'Great' (Level 5) leaders who displayed a unique balance of humility and determination that inspired their organisations and their people to achieve great results.

An interesting description of Level 5 leadership is the concept of mirror and window. When things are going well a Level 4 leader looks in the mirror and takes the credit for success. When things are not going well they look out of the window at their teams to focus the blame.

This is the opposite of a Level 5 manager. When things are going poorly they look in the mirror and take accountability, and when things are going well they look out of the window and attribute success to their teams.

Case study: Inspirational leader Professor Halina Rubinsztein-Dunlop

2018 Order of Australia recipient Professor Halina Rubinsztein-Dunlop espouses the principle of 'walking the talk' to inspire others.

Coming from the male-dominated world of physics, she has not only achieved heights of her own but also inspired others to follow their dreams.

In her youth, Professor Rubinsztein-Dunlop didn't recognise or question the unconscious bias towards women exhibited by society, however reflectively this became apparent and she realised that she could help and promote women. She received her AO for distinguished service to: laser physics and nano-optics as a researcher, mentor and academic, and for the promotion of educational programs and women in science.

Professor Rubinsztein-Dunlop firmly believes that seeing is believing. Other women in science facing their own challenges have seen her follow and achieve her dreams. As a result they had the belief that their own dreams were achievable too. They were inspired and empowered by watching her walk the talk.

Professor Rubinsztein-Dunlop had a clear vision and mission, believing her duty as a researcher and teacher was to teach the next generation. She wanted to see more women achieve and she started mentoring them. She achieved this through talking to them; demonstrating from her own merits what achievement meant; and axiomatically validating for them better self-awareness and self-worth.

One of her high potential students was finding the stress of her current situation overwhelming and as a result left her studies. Professor Rubinsztein-Dunlop followed up on her and encouraged her to re-evaluate her situation. She showed her that the door was still open to return and encouraged her to envisage the realisation of her dream. The student recognised she was capable of achieving her dream through Professor Rubinsztein-Dunlop's 'specificity versus general appraisal technique', and a 'pat on the shoulder with evidence'.

Professor Rubinsztein-Dunlop is aware of the unconscious bias that women are subjected to from her own experiences, and has been influential; she has been involved in working on panels to work towards gender equity and diversity; and she is a moderator of SAGE in Australia. She believes in good mentoring, through use of influencing and positive reinforcement, and in influencing by being a role model.

Her values were instilled in her from her own mother, who taught her to follow her dreams.

When she mentors, Professor Rubinsztein-Dunlop advocates that you should do what you really want to do; *if it's a dream, how would you do it?* And to follow the dream.

NEW RULES – 20TH CENTURY LEADERS AND 21ST CENTURY EMPLOYEES

Many leaders – perhaps even *most* leaders – struggle to inspire others. Yet, according to a survey conducted by Bain Research[7] employees are more than twice as productive if they are 'satisfied' employees. This suggests leaders who can inspire might provide a powerful competitive edge for their organisations.

In a similar vein, Harvard Business School gathered data from the assessments of more than 50,000 leaders, and the ability to inspire stood out as one of the most important competencies. It was the single trait that created the highest levels of staff engagement, and it was what separated the best leaders from everyone else. Crucially, it was what employees wanted to see most in their leaders.

It's not surprising that the ability to inspire others is such an elusive leadership attribute when you consider that most of today's corporate managers developed their management practices and habits within the constructs of the 20th century workplace.

Today's leaders often lack the playbook to inspire today's workforce, which is increasingly made up of employees who expect more meaning and value from their workplace. Whereas today's leaders have typically cut their teeth in the workplace of the 20th century, today's employees are increasingly products of the 21st century!

The critical question in attempting to offer solutions to this apparent generational leadership dilemma is: *how do today's leaders inspire the people they lead?*

Here are six ways that leaders can bridge this generational divide:

1. **Be passionate about the vision and the mission of the organisation.** Sharing a vision and mission in a way that enables others to feel passionate is a useful starting point when inspiring staff. The vision and the mission provide essential anchors for empowering others to feel that their work has a purpose and meaning beyond everyday tasks. When a leader communicates the big picture regularly it can assist in reinforcing the reason the organisation exists.

2. **Listen to your employees.** People need to see their ideas being incorporated into the team and into the organisation and/or they need to understand the reasons they weren't adopted. The ability to inspire others is not only about doing; it's about listening and explaining.

3. **Make people feel included.** Feeling inspired is about feeling connected to the actions and processes that lead to the achievement of the organisation's goals or to the decisions that are made. When a leader includes people in the decision-making process they feel a sense of ownership of that decision.

4. **Demonstrate integrity at all times.** While vision and passion are important, employees must also trust a leader. Trust stems from seeing that a leader's behaviour is aligned to what they say. Inspiring leaders walk the talk! They speak and live by their values and behave ethically. Leaders set the pace through expectations and example.

5. **Establish an environment of continuous improvement.** This includes providing opportunities for employees to grow and develop, both personally and professionally, and can be achieved by setting goals and targets, allowing for secondments to other parts of the business, establishing special projects or encouraging further study.

6. **Recognise achievement.** While financial reward is undoubtedly a significant motivator, recognition plays a vital role in making employees feel important and appreciated. Indeed, research has shown that a key source of inspiration for employees is speaking directly to them about the value of their work to the organisation.[8]

Inspirational leadership strategies

Marissa Levin's study of inspirational leadership points to eight clear strategies that inspiring leaders typically deploy.[9] They need to have a clear vision, mission and values system, and be able to articulate these so followers have something tangible to grasp. They have to create stretch goals, something that employees and followers can visualise and aspire to achieve.

Inspiring leaders work with their teams; two of the most inspiring words they use are *we* and *together*. They encourage growth in their followers, inspiring them to develop intellectually, emotionally and spiritually.

Finally, inspiring leaders acknowledge those they lead, making them feel as if they belong and they matter, and they are making a difference.

Neuroscience expert Christine Comaford questions whether leaders are scaring their employees into mediocrity. She asserts that 90% of our behaviours are driven by our emotional brain, with our intellect controlling only 10% of our decision-making. She believes that inspiring leaders:

- **Invest time in good communication.** They understand the impact of great communication and the harm of poor communication. They know communication can be a catalyst to growth, and they use it as a strategic tool to achieve their goals.

- **Listen.** Employees want to know that they matter. It's not enough to share your vision. Followers want to contribute their ideas and perspectives as well.

- **Act with integrity; inspire trust**. Employees take their cues from their leaders, they are always watching. For employees to believe in their leaders, they must *believe them*. Inspiring leaders know every action matters, whether it is in times of success or times of conflict.

Two leaders who have captured many of the strategies discussed in Marissa Levin's study are Mike Cannon-Brookes and Scott Farquhar, founders of Atlassian Corporation, an Australian enterprise software company.

Their vision was to develop software that could be used universally, scaled and replicated and, rather than requiring a dedicated sales team, would sell itself.

Their company develops products for software developers, project managers and content management, their goal being to satisfy the appetites of software creators. Their products include Jira (for issue or bug tracking for software development) and Confluence (for team collaboration and wiki).

Atlassian started with a $10,000 credit card debt in 2001, and is now valued at over $US14 billion. It services over 60,000 customers including NASA, Spotify, BMW, eBay and Coca-Cola.

In a defining moment for global teamwork, Scott Farquhar notably said:

> 'I am awed and humbled to see our dream of empowering teams all over the world come to life. It's a world that can feel pretty fragmented these days – with a complex workforce, scattered information, geopolitical silos, a growing trust gap, and so much more. We believe teams are the way forward. They are the superheroes that can bridge these divides by creating, innovating, and affecting change like never before.'

THE IMPORTANCE OF RHETORIC IN INSPIRATIONAL LEADERSHIP

Charismatic leaders demonstrate that rhetoric is a key aspect of their approach to leadership and of their success as leaders.

Communication that contains specific content references and rhetorical devices, and uses specific non-verbal behaviours in its delivery, has the capacity to profoundly influence a person's evaluation of the leader. Specifically, rhetoric can be both a significant motivator and a source of strong, positive emotions.[10]

The positive effects of charismatic leaders have been well researched:[11] political leaders including Adolf Hitler, Theodore Roosevelt and Bill Clinton; business leaders such as Lee Iacocca, Steve Jobs, Richard Branson and Anita Roddick; leaders of social revolution such as Gandhi and Martin Luther King and even terrorist leaders like Osama Bin Laden.

Each of these leaders – for better or worse – is characterised as possessing an ability to inspire and engage the desired motives of followers, arouse follower emotions and communicate a vision in terms that are meaningful to their followers. Each understands (or understood) the importance of rhetoric in leadership.

This leadership rhetoric typically includes five key components:[12]

1. **The articulation of an idealised vision.** This is generally ideological, providing or hinting at the promise of a better existence for followers whose values coincide with those of the leader. This vision serves to align the ambitions of followers with those of the organisation and the leader, and to challenge and inspire followers by arousing motivation for accomplishment of organisational goals.[13]

2. **Specific verbal references (or cues) which aim to frame the vision in a meaningful way.** Often this involves boosting the self-esteem of the audience or justifying a vision on the basis of moral values, or facilitating group identification.

3. **Specific rhetorical techniques.** These might include:
    - References to specific (often historical) people
    - Frequent use of the word 'us'
    - Aspirational references – such as to 'hopes and dreams'
    - A refusal to use a script, speech notes or prompter.

    Rhetorical techniques assist in framing the vision and engaging the attention, emotions and motives of the audience. These techniques help to capture audience attention and result in more positive impressions of the leader.[14]

4. **The use of non-verbal behaviours.** Specifically, eye contact and interjections by the speaker, variety in vocal tone and fluency, and animated gestures – smiling, positive head nods – contribute to audience involvement and more favourable impressions of the speaker.[15] Similarly, vocal and facial pleasantness and relaxed posture were found to impact on speaker credibility and persuasiveness.[16]

5. **Visible personal attributes.** Charismatic leaders are often defined as leaders with exceptional qualities and abilities demonstrated in the manifestation of personal traits such as confidence and high self-esteem.[17]

Leadership action

When Howard Schultz returned to Starbucks as CEO he realised that Starbucks' unique customer-focused coffee experience was in the back seat, automation and diversification having taken over. He changed the company's direction; he shut down 7,100 US stores for three hours on February 26th, 2008, to retrain the baristas in the art of making expresso, leaving no doubt about his intentions.[18]

THE LEADER'S ROLE IN DRIVING MOTIVATION AND ENGAGEMENT

Motivation

While some organisational psychologists have different opinions about what is most effective when it comes to motivating a team, few would argue that all team members are motivated by the same things.

What this means for us as leaders is that we must invest time in getting to know our teams and learning about their drivers and motivators. One size doesn't fit all, and the ability to recognise this – and to act on it on a daily basis – is the first step on the road to becoming an inspirational leader. One person's 'rah-rah', happy-clappy motivational session is another person's idea of acute embarrassment.

It's important to recognise that a team of people is made up of different personalities, backgrounds, experiences, educations, cultural histories and all manner of other factors. Indeed, often it is only the fact that your team works for the same company at the same time that is the single thing they have in common. But it is that very fact that can prove to be the foundation upon which inspirational leadership is built.

A good starting point is to ask your team members, *'What do you like most about working here?'* And, *'What would make this the perfect place to work?'*

Answers to these types of questions (and similar) can provide valuable insights into what motivates each member of your team. Our role as leader isn't to seek sameness and uniformity, it is to understand what drives different people to perform at their best. A leader's role is to create the environment where employees feel motivated to achieve their best.

While it's true that employees are typically motivated by very different things, studies of motivation and employee engagement have found that there are 'typical' aspects of a leadership style and a work environment that can serve to drive staff engagement and employee motivation. Broadly, these fall into five areas:

1. **Control and responsibility.** Control of their work inspires motivation: including such components as the ability to have an impact on decisions; setting clear and measurable goals; clear responsibility for a complete, or at least defined, task; job enrichment; tasks performed in the work itself; and recognition for achievement.

2. **Management sharing information.** Being informed creates motivation: including receiving timely information and communication; understanding management's reasons for decision-making; team and meeting participation opportunities.

3. **Growth and development.** The opportunity for growth and development is motivational: it includes education and training; career paths; team participation; succession planning and cross-function training.

4. **Consistent leadership.** Leadership is key in motivation. People want clear expectations that provide a picture of the outcomes desired from goal-setting and feedback and an appropriate structure or framework.

5. **Recognition.** People want recognition for their individual performance. They want to be acknowledged and to feel that their organisation appreciates their efforts.

These areas might provide a reasonable starting point for a leader looking to explore the individual motivators of their teams. Once you have an understanding of each team member's personal drivers – the things that will serve to increase engagement – you can start to implement strategies, policies, processes and activities that tap into each of these. At the very least, you will have greater understanding of why your staff act in a certain way or say certain things in specific situations.

Engagement

Like motivation, engagement is an important aspect of inspirational leadership. Unfortunately, these days engagement has become synonymous with the (often dreaded) annual employee engagement survey within an organisation.

It wasn't always that way. There is a gradual realisation among leaders and within organisations that engagement is far more – and far more important – than the annual survey of employees.

Employee engagement refers to the emotional commitment between an employee and their workplace. Highly engaged employees are positively committed to doing their best to help their organisations grow.

Inspirational leaders typically lead highly engaged teams and organisations. They understand the need for an ongoing commitment to, and continuous dialogue about, engagement levels. Of course, an annual survey that is focused on establishing a benchmark against which to measure engagement can be an important starting point, but it isn't the 'be all and end all'. Far more critical is the establishment of an ongoing commitment to employee engagement.

A leadership commitment to engagement might include the following:

1. Comprehensive induction processes that include reference to the vision and mission of the business to ensure that employees understand where the business is headed and why it is going in that direction.

2. Regular strategy updates, reviews and re-sets with senior leaders. These serve to instil and cement trust in the senior leadership team.

3. The implementation of formal and informal feedback processes. These might include 360-degree feedback tools and other similar surveys that serve to focus on the empowerment of staff.

4. Input mechanisms that allow staff to add to the strategic direction and operational plans of the business, for example ideas sessions, strategy off-sites, planning days, suggestion boxes and their online equivalents. These serve to allow staff to have input into the direction of the business.

5. A holistic approach to learning and development. This will illustrate to staff that their development is on the leader's radar and is important to the business.

6. A clear approach to reward and recognition. It is important that employees know how they are rewarded and recognised and what the leader's expectations are in terms of reward and recognition. Nothing destroys engagement faster than a confused and inconsistent approach to reward and recognition from the leader.

7. A clear approach to and view about workplace culture. This is especially true when it comes to the sort of behaviour that is viewed as being acceptable and that which isn't. Inspirational leaders tend to be very clear about this and about calling out poor behaviour as soon as they see it.

As the leader of a team you want to know if your team is engaged. Although some organisations use staff engagement surveys to quantify the levels of engagement across the organisation, the simplest way is to observe your team and look for signs of the following:

- **Learning** – are your staff developing and learning new skills?
- **Helping** – do your staff help each other regularly?
- **Making suggestions** – do they make suggestions to help improve the organisation or the customer experience?
- **Sharing** – do they feel confident to share their feelings or concerns with you?

INSPIRING YOURSELF!

All this discussion about the need for modern leaders to possess the ability to inspire others ignores one very simple and important question: how do you keep your head up and stay motivated yourself? As a leader, how do you remain inspired?

The simple fact is that it is impossible to inspire others if you yourself are not inspired. If you're 'not feeling it' you can't expect your team to feel it!

As the leader, you set the tone for the team to follow. If you are feeling unmotivated or negative then, chances are, this will be reflected by your team. Inspirational leaders intuitively know that they must 'walk the talk', but if that walk is more of a deflated hobble, what can we do to return the spring to our step?

It is important that leaders are mindful and proactive at managing their own motivations and ensuring that they are aware of their own feelings and motivation levels. Self-awareness is a key aspect of a leader's ability to inspire others.

There are several actions you can take to help you re-energise and keep yourself engaged, motivated and inspired.

- **Revisit your 'why'** – Take a step back and focus on what you want to achieve in both your career and your personal life. Try to remind yourself why you do what you do. What is most important to you and how can you align your work and personal time with achieving this?

- **Take regular breaks** – Taking time off away from work is a successful way to re-energise and recharge. All leadership roles have elements of stress and anxiety and so it's important to recognise the need to take time away from work to help you rebuild.

- **Set personal challenges** – Identify some new goals and projects you can work on which will give you a true sense of satisfaction. These could include learning new skills, taking on new roles or being involved in projects or committees outside of your normal comfort zone. Set a goal and a deadline and then work towards achieving it.

- **Look for new ways of doing things** – Challenge the status quo and invest time and effort in trying to find better ways of doing things. Here you might look for innovation and ideas that can save time and costs or improve quality. There might also be ways to improve tasks to make them easier and more enjoyable.

A simple checklist for leaders to measure their ability to inspire

The following model enables you as team leader to identify and address some of the key factors to building an inspired and engaged team.

1. **Task needs.** Ensuring the team understand and are committed to the tasks they are doing.
2. **Team needs.** Ensuring the team is functioning and supporting each other as team members
3. **Individual needs.** Ensuring each individual knows their role and expectations within the team.

Task needs

- ☐ Do I understand the team's objectives?
- ☐ Have I communicated the objectives to the team?
- ☐ Have I prioritised each task?
- ☐ Do we have adequate resources?
- ☐ Do we have a timeline to achieve our tasks?
- ☐ Do I have measuring systems in place?
- ☐ Do we have the right skills in the team?
- ☐ Have the tasks been allocated to the right people?
- ☐ Does everyone know who should be doing what?

Team needs

- ☐ Does the team understand the goals?
- ☐ Have performance standards been set?
- ☐ Have behaviour standards been set?
- ☐ Do I have the right mix of people?
- ☐ What is the morale of the team?
- ☐ Is conflict dealt with appropriately?
- ☐ Are there regular team briefings?
- ☐ Do the team members share their skills and knowledge?
- ☐ How quickly do I find out about problems?
- ☐ Do we celebrate achievements together?

Individual needs

- ☐ Does each individual know their targets?
- ☐ Do I speak with them individually?
- ☐ Do I know their personal career goals?
- ☐ Do they know how their work fits in to the overall result?
- ☐ Do they have a clear job description?
- ☐ Do I review their performance regularly?
- ☐ How do they deal with conflict?
- ☐ How satisfied are they with their job?
- ☐ What are their strengths and weaknesses?

TUCKMAN'S TEAM DEVELOPMENT MODEL

The Team Development Cycle is a useful tool to help leaders engage with their teams and develop them into an effective unit. The model was designed by Bruce Tuckman in 1965 (see Figure 4.2). As you can see from the figure, there are five stages to the model: forming, storming, norming, performing and adjourning.

Figure 4.2 – Tuckman's Team Development Cycle

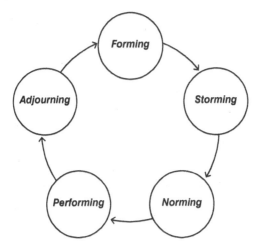

In the forming stage, you have a group of people with a range of personalities. Some will be positive, some anxious, others excited, etc., about the task facing the new team. It is not until they start working together, get to know each other and settle into the roles they play that the team can move on to 'storming'. This first stage can take some time as the individual and collective responsibilities and goals of the team are worked out. At the forming stage, as a leader, you should outline your expectations and be clear about each person's objectives and roles and responsibilities.

When the team moves into the storming phase, conflicts can emerge, authority can be challenged and the work might seem overwhelming. At this stage, there is the greatest risk that the team may fail. There are many reasons why this happens. The leader might not have clearly set the goals in the forming stage, conflicts may not have been addressed and nipped in the bud, and there may not have been enough time to build trust. Leaders must remain positive and encourage the team to work hard, stick with the task at hand and work through the challenges.

When the team reaches the third stage, people start to resolve their differences, appreciate colleagues' strengths and respect the authority of the leader. Team members may have started to socialise better, build mutual trust and be more comfortable asking for help and taking feedback. There is now a strong commitment towards the team's goal.

Now in its fourth stage the team is really firing – it's performing! Systems and processes are working. The leader knows their team better and is comfortable delegating more, and everyone feels part of the team as they work hard to achieve their objectives.

Tuckman added the fifth stage 'adjourning' at a later stage. It is sometimes known as the 'mourning' stage because team members who like routine, or who have developed close working relationships with colleagues, may find this stage difficult, particularly if their future now looks uncertain.

The adjourning stage is inevitable though, because project teams exist for a fixed timeframe or to achieve an agreed goal, then they are disbanded. One way to soften the breakup of the team is to celebrate its achievements.

An inspirational leader who is familiar with Tuckman's model will find it easier to lead the team as it morphs through the five stages.

As a team leader, your aim is to help your people perform well, as quickly as possible. To do this, you'll need to change your approach at each stage.

You can follow the steps below to ensure that you're doing the right thing at the right time:

1. Identify the stage of team development that your team is at from the descriptions above.
2. Consider what you need to do to move towards the performing stage.
3. Schedule regular reviews of where your team is and adjust your behaviour and leadership approach appropriately.

THE FINAL WORD ON THE ABILITY TO INSPIRE

There can be little doubt that we are living (and working) in the era of inspirational leadership. Vision, passion and an ability to inspire others is the order of the day and today's leaders are expected to possess that 'special something' – the ability to inspire.

Great results can be achieved by employees who work not just for financial reward but also for the ability to do something they find inspiring. Inspirational leaders are becoming the 'norm' and the ability to inspire is increasingly becoming the focus of the leadership recruitment process and performance appraisal.

The shift from simple product benefits to a more holistic (and less 'solid') customer experience as a major source of competitive advantage means that frontline workers determine not just the quality of the customer experience but have more far-reaching effects. Just as the workplace itself has changed, so has the nature of work itself. There is an ever-increasing requirement for collaboration and teamwork – often across countries, time zones and cultures. The ability to operate in, thrive in and inspire in this brave new world of work is increasingly an essential part of modern leadership.

In the 21st century workplace leaders can no longer rely on the traditional motivation tools. The carrot and stick approach is long gone and is unlikely to return any time soon. Modern leaders must have the ability to energise their employees, foster engagement and create a trusting atmosphere – and inspire.

The ability to inspire others is now an essential ingredient in attracting and retaining the best talent. Inspirational leaders possess a clear vision, mission and values system. They have the desire and the ability to communicate these fundamentals in a clear, consistent and enthusiastic manner. However, it's more than the ability to communicate effectively that lies at the heart of a leader's ability to inspire. Inspirational leaders recognise the importance of listening to their people. They demonstrate integrity and view themselves as role models in the workplace.

Inspirational leadership is learned experientially – the skills need to be practised, lived and felt. This may involve embracing new ways of interacting, reflecting on their impact and revising your approach at times. Developing an inspirational rhetoric using inspirational language is an important facet.

The ability to inspire isn't innate, it can be developed, honed and improved.

Chapter 5

AUTHENTICITY

Allison Keogh

Happiness is when what you think,
what you say and what you do
is in harmony.

Mahatma Gandhi

Author note

I consider authenticity to be a devilishly difficult leadership attribute.

An enjoyable aspect of my role as the Chief Executive at one of the most respected management and leadership Institutes in the region is that I regularly present on leadership topics and trends. In one of my presentations (The Six Layers of Intentional Leadership) I talk about the difficulty I have with authentic leadership. I ask the question: when it comes to good leadership, is authenticity enough? Surely, sound leadership requires the leader to be more than authentic?

I can think of no better leader to answer this question and to tackle this topic than Allison Keogh.

I first met Allison when I worked for CanTeen, the iconic Australian youth cancer charity. I led the Marketing, Communications and Fundraising Team and I consider this to be the role that really began to shape and define my personal leadership style and approach. Allison was a management and leadership consultant who had – and still has – a real passion for giving back to the community. She was retained on a pro-bono basis to assist CanTeen's leadership team with our personal and professional development.

The personal leadership journey I embarked on with Allison's guidance continues today. It's safe to say that for me it was career defining. Allison taught me the immense value that can come from seeking and receiving feedback and in changing your approach to your own leadership on the basis of that feedback.

In this chapter Allison expands on this theme. She places authenticity at the very heart of the journey of self-discovery and change that leadership should be. She also tackles head-on what she considers to be the 'dark side' of authenticity.

Reflecting on this chapter as I did when I first read Allison's approach to the topic of authentic leadership, I'm delighted to say that yet again Allison has caused me to stop and reflect.

Authentic leadership – as defined here – is a crucial attribute for today's leader and it's one that is quite rightly included in this book.

WHEN IT COMES to authenticity, Oscar Wilde famously quipped, *'Be yourself; everyone else is already taken'*. This suggests that we'll be just fine if we simply *be ourselves*. But is this true? Is it really that simple? Is authenticity about 'just being yourself' and allowing people to get to know you?

As a leader and coach, I have closely observed the birth and subsequent evolution of a myriad leadership theories. Leadership was once considered to be primarily 'transactional'. It was simply a function of organising people, supervising them and managing their performance. It was about maintaining the status quo and staying the course. Leaders were there simply to manage the resources (including the people) that the company deemed to be in need of management! In these terms, leaders were really managers with a fancy name that made them sound less transactional than they really were.

The rise and dominance of the concept of 'charismatic' leadership saw a shift in emphasis from transaction to inspiration. Inspiring people rather than simply managing them became the order of the day, and an entire industry based around motivational theory and practice began to take root and bloom. At its heart, this industry (and I am unapologetically one of its most ardent proponents) places persuading and influencing people through conviction and vision as the primary means by which leaders lead. They are the key reasons why we choose to 'follow the leader'.

More recently, a new layer of leadership has been added. Transformational leadership is founded on the concept of challenging followers, identifying a need for change and building followers into future leaders, who themselves create change and progress. The role of the leader has become one of leading others to lead.

Encouraging people to think for themselves, challenge themselves and challenge the leader has produced a new wave of expectation. Transformational leadership when overlaid on top of a modern, talented workforce can be seen to be leading to increased expectations and demands. In short, people are no longer so easily persuaded and so quick to follow. In the modern workplace, people want to *align* themselves with people, rather than simply *follow* them.

Alignment, agreement and consensus have become the key drivers and in turn, for leaders especially, trust and believability are now the major currencies of the modern workplace. This change has been profound; nowhere more so than in the boardrooms and corner offices with their expensive vistas of the leadership floors. People now need (demand!) to know their leader and the organisation they work for on a much more personal and purposeful level, requiring a higher level of transparency about who their leader is, what they stand for, and how authentically they deliver on their promises.

Can you see the real me? Aligning intent and impact

As a young a project manager, I was tasked with leading a team of university graduates. I relished the responsibility of seeing them grow, learn, contribute and build confidence in their work life. A few months into my stint as their leader, I underwent a leadership development program involving feedback from the team.

I was fully expecting rave reviews, but the truth is that the results shocked and upset me. While I received relatively positive feedback about my focus on achieving results, my team were less than impressed with my leadership style. They found me to be hypercritical, unrealistic in my demands and overly directive.

This was my first experience of the power of feedback. I found myself at a leadership crossroad – my first leadership crossroad. I knew that I needed to reflect on how I *thought* I needed to be. My leadership style was based on looking the part: I dressed in a power suit and I had adopted 'a tough persona'. I felt that this was what it meant to be a project manager. I had formed the view that project managers were the efficient, competent, task masters and that to be a successful project manager I needed to be the tenacious, professional tough chick, who could be relied on to be decisive and in control.

The funny thing is this: I knew it was a mask. Those close to me in my personal life described me differently. Outside of work – when I wasn't 'Allison the Project Manager', I was described as someone who was encouraging, collaborative and supportive. My friends said that I always had a clear desire to connect with people and to understand other people's points of view and perspectives. I can clearly remember a good friend of mine telling me that she felt I sounded like a different person if she ever phoned me at work. She said I was short, abrupt and business-like, while outside of work I was funny, fun and light-hearted.

In addition to these things that I thought I needed to *be* at work, were the things that I thought I needed to *do* to get the best out of my team. I freely admit that I did monitor their work closely (in my mind at least) to prevent them from making mistakes. I did critique their work (in my mind at least) to help them to 'take it to the next level'. I gave them (what I thought was) constant 'advice' and loads of direction.

The result of all this was that they felt that nothing was ever good enough. They also felt that I didn't trust them and that I wasn't open to their ideas. Rather than 'Allison the super leader' growing their confidence, I was eroding it.

While the obvious first step was to drop the mask and the persona of the 'Tenacious Tough Chick', there was another thing I needed to focus on: alignment. My *intent* and my *impact* were worlds apart. I had succeeded in creating an inauthentic result.

Being authentic is about more than just 'being yourself'; it's about what we do to create alignment between our intent and impact. This is depicted in Figure 5.1.

Figure 5.1 – Impact and intent: what we want, what we create and what we get

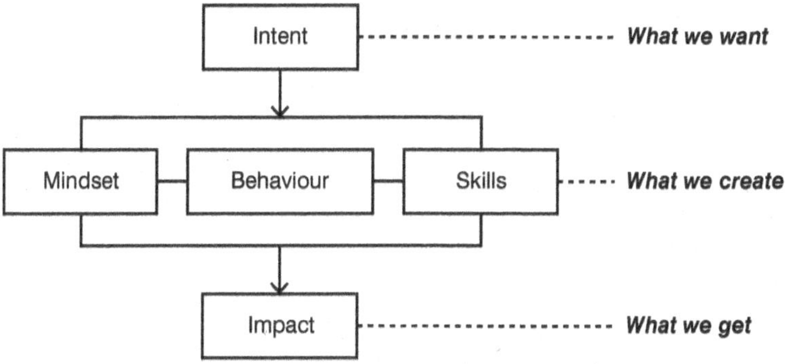

THE HEAVY COST OF NOT BEING AUTHENTIC

As I discovered as a project manager, you pay a significant cost for not being authentic. It's too easy to measure that cost in terms of the impact on your team. Of course, there is no denying that this impact is great, and can be incredibly damaging. Team morale can slip, the team can and often does break up, people leave, others join and then they leave. In short, staff turnover increases. These things, while clearly important, are external. There are other costs to count, and you feel these much closer to home.

I wonder if some of these ring true for you?

Judgement

One such cost is facing judgement. The irony of this is not lost on me. We often don't show our true, authentic selves for fear of being judged. But failing to be authentic means that people make assumptions about us based on our behaviour and impact.

One of the best illustrations of this is a process I use when delivering change leadership training. Invariably, a client requests learning for leaders to deal with their biggest challenge: resistance to change.

First, I ask participants to outline the reasons *other* people resist change. The reasons usually include some assessment of negative intent. The person resisting change is simply 'change resistant', sabotaging, they dislike change itself or are acting in self-interest.

Then, I ask why they *themselves* may have not embraced a particular change. Responses tend to include more external factors, such as the change being badly managed, there being no obvious or justifiable reason for the change, a lack of consultation, poor communication or the impact had not properly been assessed.

We often habitually and unconsciously judge ourselves by our intent, but judge others by their behaviour and impact. If we fail to reveal and align ourselves, we will face that judgement.

Trade-offs

The second cost of not being authentic is the trade-offs we make.

Being faced with dilemmas is the greatest challenge to authenticity we will ever have, and it's a true test of our values.

Many of us have experience of working with a team member who was causing enormous damage. One that springs to mind for me was an experience of harassment, bullying, intimidation, undermining and manipulation. It was toxic. It affected me and others deeply. It created an environment of low trust and an extraordinary amount of wasted energy and stress. My manager was a terrific person – a believer in civility, equality and respect. However, he only acted on it after two of us resigned.

Sometime later he approached me to have a conversation about what went on and he acknowledged the cost of his inaction. It hadn't been the first time he had failed to take timely action in similar circumstances. To his credit, he wanted to personally reflect and make change. When we explored it, he arrived at the conclusion he was avoiding discomfort, conflict and the consequences of tackling an aggressive person who wielded so much power and influence. He was trading off! What he hadn't considered was that the consequences of the trade-offs he was making were his own values and the wellbeing of the other staff.

Ultimately, he ended up learning that being inauthentic can lead to trading off things that are actually important to you.

Energy

Ah, energy – that thing that we crave, that we wish we had more of! Actually, maybe it's that thing that we would have more of if we weren't misaligned.

Adopting a persona and managing our reactions and behaviour is exhausting. Behaving in a way that is inauthentic depletes us. At one end of the spectrum sits the energy involved in expressing strong emotional reactions. At the other end is the energy required to suppress them and censor ourselves. This energy could be spent more productively. Being yourself is easy, trying to be someone you're not isn't.

The cost of inauthenticity is both internal and external. Internally, it creates anxiety, stress, exhaustion and internal conflict. Externally, it creates judgement, a lack of trust and believability. It takes work to create alignment, but the reward is greater energy, satisfaction and integrity.

Revealing me! Creating alignment

So, back to the devastating feedback I received as a project manager.

Just being aware of the impact I was having on the team wasn't enough. I knew that I needed to give serious consideration to my intent and to the legacy I wanted to leave as a leader.

I sat down with my team members and asked them for more specific feedback about how I impacted them and what I was doing to create that impact. This wasn't an easy thing to do. It required me to shift my mindset and then my behaviour to align with my intent. It also meant that I needed to begin a process of self-reflection. Ultimately, it required me to develop new leadership skills, tools and techniques to be more effective.

My entire way of developing team members underwent a profound shift. I reserved 'teaching' people for when it was genuinely needed and focused my efforts on nurturing their talents, welcoming their ideas and recognising their potential. Crucially, I was told that I needed to delegate more and to trust my team members. What they really wanted was coaching, not directing.

This was my first introduction to the concept of the leader as a coach as opposed to the leader acting as a manager who directs the team. I was expected to show encouragement and respect for the team's ideas and their solutions (which, not surprisingly, often proved to be better than mine!). I was also expected to evaluate the work of the team members based on outcomes rather than some vague notion that I had of perfection.

Instead of believing that I needed to be the holder of all knowledge, I made a personal commitment to lifelong learning and to continual development.

Authenticity means redefining your role

Looking back and reflecting on my experience as a young project manager, what I actually did (what I needed to do) was to redefine the role of 'project manager'. I had defined my role in a certain way and I was executing that role to meet that definition. But isn't this exactly what we tend to do? We tend to believe that a lawyer is typically X or an accountant is typically Y. We assign certain characteristics to roles and to entire professions and then we expect the people doing those roles to fit the bill.

As a project manager, I was supposed to be focused on a rigid structure of task management and delivery. I was supposed to drive the team task by task, chart by chart and day by day. I was supposed to manage them closely to ensure that the project didn't slip or (horror of horrors!) veer off track completely. If it did, I was the project manager, and it was my head on the block.

My own definition of a project manager at the time wasn't one that encouraged personal growth, learning, innovation, flexibility, collaboration and progress.

The feedback from my team caused me to rethink all of this dramatically. Fundamentally, it caused me to question my definition of what a project manager is and does. It wasn't that I questioned whether I was a good task manager. What I questioned was how I did the role, and whether I could achieve the same (or better) results by doing it differently; by being different; by being me. It certainly seemed to be what the team wanted. I had heard that loud and clear.

So, I started dressing differently at work. This meant that I began to turn up in a way that was much more comfortable to me. At the same time, I became less formal and I started to enjoy some humour with the team. Don't get me wrong, I didn't start wearing a red nose and huge clown shoes in the office, and I didn't sit with team members and engage in daily 'deep and meaningfuls'. I certainly saved my inner Dancing Queen for my friends on a Saturday night! But I did become more approachable, more connected with people and more fun to work with. If you'd have asked me previously I would absolutely have rejected 'fun' as being an essential element of the role of project manager.

The impact of this redefinition of my role – and of me – was as profound as the redefinition itself. My team began to be more open with me and, most importantly, they realised that they could let their own guard down too and be more themselves at work. But it was more than that; the team dynamic changed too. We began to make better decisions that were based on collaboration and discussion. With this different input, the quality of the output improved and the team actually achieved and delivered *more* work that was of greater value to the customer, because the team were empowered to do so.

I was still a project manager, but I was a different project manager to the one I thought I should have been. I was starting to be the kind of project manager I really wanted to be.

As you can see, authenticity is more than just trying to be yourself at work. It is not a fixed idea of how we can and should be. It requires change and redefinition. In some cases, it requires us to rethink what we've learnt about our roles and about what it takes to be successful in a role.

Over the years, I have found it an extremely useful exercise to actually write down a simple comparison between what you think you should be in your role at work and what you would be and how you would act if you weren't constrained by these preconceptions. On many occasions, I've found the results to be startling. Often this surprise leads to the start of a change process. The following checklist provides a great way to check out how you align with your role.

THE 8 STEPS TO BECOMING MORE AUTHENTIC

Sheryl Sandberg, Facebook's Chief Operating Officer, has written that, *'Leaders should strive for authenticity over perfection'*.[1] It's interesting to reflect on the amount of time we spend at work trying to do things absolutely perfectly; on getting things just right. To be truly authentic and true to your values, beliefs and intent requires just as much effort and work. It's more than just speaking your mind. It requires self-awareness, emotional intelligence and, crucially, changed behaviour.

Of course, this is no easy task. If it were easy, I'm sure that every leader would be much more authentic and leadership capability would be greatly improved. However, the fact that it's difficult means that once it is achieved there is a far greater sense of accomplishment and an impact that makes the effort worthwhile.

I like to view the journey to greater authenticity as a process. It's probably the project manager in me! In fact, I believe that this process has eight clear and definable steps. These are:

1. Crafting and sharing intent (purpose, mission, values and impact)
2. Seeking feedback
3. Self-reflection
4. Changing behaviour
5. Developing capability
6. Being discerning and adaptable

7. Being a role model

8. Feeling and accepting discomfort.

Step 1: Craft and share your intent

Step 1 involves taking the following steps to craft and share your intent.

Define your purpose

Simon Sinek's powerful TED talk, 'Start with why' went viral many years ago, and for good reason. We engage fully and are inspired to act when we have a clear reason to do so. Gaining clarification of our role as authentic leaders is a powerful motivator.

Develop your mission

What outcomes do you want to achieve? What do you want to be remembered for? What will be the lasting legacy of your time as a leader?

Clarify your values

While your purpose gives you the 'why' and the mission gives you the 'what', the values are the 'how'. These are the thoughts, beliefs and behaviours that guide you in situations of pressure or tough calls requiring you to make trade-offs.

Describe your desired impact

How will your purpose, mission and values manifest in practical, everyday impacts? What is your leadership philosophy and approach? What is the desired impact on you, your team, your organisation, customers and the community? What do you want people to say about how your leadership affects them?

Share your intent

It can be difficult to fully trust people we don't know. Clarifying and sharing our intent gives people a sense of who we are, what we stand for, what they can expect from us, and it removes assumptions about our motivation.

Step 2: Seek feedback

One of the most powerful things ever said to me was by a terrific mentor when I was anxiously awaiting some leadership survey feedback results. Sensing my trepidation, he simply said: *'if something surprises you about this feedback, you are probably the only person who doesn't know'.*

It forever shifted my attitude to seeking and receiving feedback. Rather than feeling anxious and fearful of what I might hear, I continually feel a sense of relief and gratitude. I'm simply finding out what others are thinking or saying about me at the water cooler, and I'd rather know about it. I care about the impact I have and how aligned it is with my intent and purpose.

Feedback really matters

One CEO I worked with was particularly grateful for feedback. I was a consultant engaged to develop HR strategy, systems and processes at an exciting stage of growth for the business.

Every conversation we had felt like a mental boxing match. He critiqued every idea to the point of running it down completely and asking me to justify it and 'fight' for it. When we eventually landed on an idea, I was always left with a crushing feeling that the result was still inferior.

We had plenty more work to complete together, so I decided to give him some feedback. It went something like this:

'I'd like to talk to you about my experience of working with you on this so far. You seem to be dissatisfied with whatever I produce. Our conversations focus on what is wrong with an idea, rather than working towards a solution. The impact of this is that I feel exhausted, lose motivation, productivity and any sense of satisfaction and achievement. I'm wondering why you do this? What is your thinking when you are doing this?'

What transpired was enlightening. The CEO's *intent* was to 'stimulate thinking and creativity'. He also thought that 'fighting' for an idea generates more passion for it. He believed that people performed at their best and produced superior results if they were constantly 'dissatisfied' with what they produced. His ultimate motive was to find the optimal solution. And, for the first time, he disclosed that he was thrilled with what I had come up with, but didn't want to tell me because he thought it might reduce my motivation to pursue continual improvement.

He also checked with his staff and received similar feedback. They felt exhausted after floating an idea with him. One person disclosed that they would only attempt it when they were well rested beforehand and could lay down for a nap afterwards! His impact was in complete misalignment with his intent. But he was able to adjust quickly, because he accepted the feedback in the context of his impact, without justifying his behaviour on the basis of his intent. This was critical to shift, because the business itself was built on innovation and creativity – and his impact was stifling it.

Authenticity requires the courage to face the judgement of others, and to use it for our own learning, development and growth. There can be no change without awareness, and without feedback we have limited awareness.

Being willing and able to take action following feedback requires an interim step: acceptance. One of the biggest barriers to feedback creating change is being unable to accept the feedback. In turn, one of the biggest barriers to accepting the feedback is the meaning we attach to it: that it reflects who we are and our identity – our authentic selves. Feedback is in relation to our behaviour and impact. It is important to interpret feedback as being about how *effective* we are, rather than about *who* we are (see Figure 5.2).

Figure 5.2 – The layers of personality, self concept, thinking, behaviour and impact

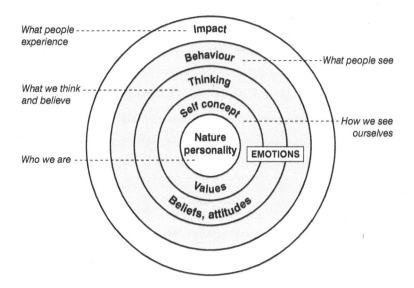

It is common for people to confuse changeable factors with their personality. We tend to get stuck thinking that our behaviour is simply a part of us. However, alignment for authenticity doesn't require changing who we are, it requires changing how we show up. It requires adopting what psychologist Carol Dweck refers to as a 'growth' mindset rather than 'fixed' mindset.

Genuine feedback can be difficult to get. As leaders, people will often tell us what they think we want to hear.

This means that it is absolutely critical you surround yourself with people who will be honest with you *and* who are interested in your success, development and growth – people who will both challenge and support you and who will hold you accountable for your impact.

Step 3: Self-reflection

'Between stimulus and response there is a space.
In that space is our power to choose our response.
In our response lies our growth and our freedom.'

Note: This quote has widely, and most likely erroneously, been attributed to Viktor Frankl. Frankl was a psychiatrist and survivor of the Holocaust. His most famous book, *Man's Search for Meaning*, certainly contains an enduring insight about the freedom in choosing a response to situations that cannot be controlled but does not contain this quote. It was perhaps popularised through Stephen Covey's work where he attributes this thinking to Frankl in his bestseller *Seven Habits of Highly Effective People*.

In a time when productivity, efficiency and decisiveness are valued, fast thinking has become the norm. This undoubtedly has its benefits and is particularly crucial in specific circumstances and emergencies. However, fast thinking can sometimes be the enemy of authenticity.

Authenticity requires us to raise our consciousness above the typical stimulus/response cycle. Often, we react to a circumstance or trigger unconsciously – in both our thoughts and emotions (see Figure 5.3). Perhaps the best-known and pioneering work in this area was done by Russian physiologist Ivan Pavlov.[2] He discovered what is now known as 'Classical Conditioning'. His most famous experiment involved sounding a metronome (or bell) when feeding a dog. After repeating this a few times, the dog would salivate at the sound of the bell, without any food being present – essentially demonstrating that certain stimuli or 'triggers' could be conditioned for a particular response by association.

Figure 5.3 – Stimulus, thought and response[3]

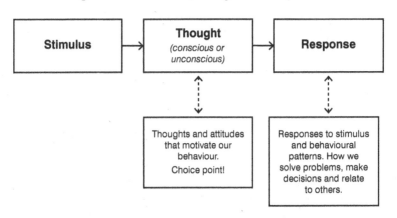

'*Every ancestor of every action is thought.*'

—Ralph Waldo Emerson

Barriers to authenticity

We tend to focus on what we need to *do* to be authentic. But first, it is helpful to actually reflect on the things that 'get in the way' of us *being* authentic. In my own leadership development – and from my experience coaching others – I have found that there are ten common barriers to being authentic:

1. **Adopting a 'persona'.** Believing we need to 'be' a certain way or adopting a stereotypical image or 'brand'.

2. **Approval.** Being how we think others want us to be, or telling them what we think they want to hear, in order to be liked, accepted or admired.

3. **Control.** Believing we need to demonstrate a sense of order and being in control. Censoring ourselves and our emotions. Thinking we can control how others see us.

4. **Perfection.** Striving for perfection and wanting to appear competent, knowledgeable and capable.

5. **Comparison.** Comparing ourselves to other people in order to feel adequate, worthy or better. Defining who we are or how we should be, based on how others are.

6. **Conformity.** A desire to 'fit in', comply with norms and blend in.

7. **Comfort.** Not standing up for what we believe or avoiding facing the tough issues due to discomfort.

8. **Fear.** Fear of the consequences of speaking up or being ourselves – consequences such as conflict, rejection, judgement and exclusion.

9. **Self-awareness.** Unconscious beliefs, attitudes and behaviours and impact on people. Unconscious bias based on preferences and experiences.

10. **Capability.** Not developing the right skills, tools and techniques, believing we can just act on instincts.

Self-reflection is about slowing down our thinking and allowing ourselves the time to understand what associations we make and the reasons for our reactions and actions. In her book *Change your Thinking*[4] psychologist Dr Sarah Edelman suggests responding to unhelpful or limiting thoughts with positive rebuttals. For example, in response to a desire for approval, we could say: 'Not all people will like me, and that's OK'; 'People will actually approve of me more if I speak more truthfully.'

Monitoring and challenging our thoughts and associated emotions can actually provide us with greater freedom to be ourselves by removing the barriers of unhelpful thinking.

Step 4: Change behaviour

We are sometimes asked to change our behaviour to have a more constructive impact, but what if that behaviour doesn't come naturally to us?

It's important to understand that all behaviour is learned. We aren't born with a certain set of reactions – other than the very basic survival instincts. However, we come to feel comfortable with behaviours that we have learned over a period of time. Learning new behaviours restarts and resets this process of learning. Of course, this is often something very new because we have always behaved and reacted in a certain way at certain times. It's true that 'new' can feel uncomfortable and unnatural and can prevent us from changing.

What if our beliefs and attitudes are inconsistent with the behaviour? Can we authentically change behaviour if it doesn't align with what we think?

I'm a boss, not a friend

One leader I worked with as a coach experienced these challenges. He had received feedback that people felt he didn't show enough genuine interest in them.

In the coaching session, he disclosed his current mindset. He didn't want to get to know his people – he was their manager, not their friend! He wasn't there for any kind of social club and he wanted to keep work life and private life separate. He wasn't interested in their lives and didn't want to pretend to be.

I admired his honesty. How many times have we had a leader ask us *'How was your weekend?'*, only for them to glaze over when we start to respond.

So, I asked him what he was interested in about his team members – and things he could develop genuine interest in. We tapped into something. He cared about how they did their work and how successful and valued they felt they were.

The first step was to explore a way that he could authentically start to show interest in his team as people. Rather than asking people how their weekend was or about their personal interests, he started showing interest in how they were feeling about their work, what challenges they were having, how much they were enjoying it, what they gained satisfaction from. He could do that genuinely. Interactions moved from being simply transactional to being much more relational.

Our next step on this leader's journey involved what organisational psychologist, Adam Grant (referencing the work of sociologist Arlie Hochschild) might call 'deep acting'[5]. So, instead of the leader carrying out the exhausting work of 'surface acting', I encouraged him to leverage his feelings of genuine interest in their work to something more; to ask questions such as *'How was your weekend?'*, but in a state of deep acting.

What transpired was telling.

He was genuinely fascinated and excited about all the new information he learned about his team. He felt closer to his colleagues, understood them and trusted them more. But he didn't learn these things through simply faking it. His 'deep acting' actually created a genuine interest.

This leader now 'identifies' himself as someone who is genuinely interested in people, because he created a new and positive experience through a change in behaviour. Sometimes, it's good to 'try something on'.

Source: Grant, A. M. (2013) 'Rocking the boat but keeping it steady: The role of emotional regulation in employee voice', *Academy of Management Journal*, Vol 56. No. 6. 1703-1723

Changing behaviour can actually result in a changed mindset and an altered concept of our self (see Figure 5.4). When we create new experiences, we make new associations, and our change in thinking and behaviour becomes natural and permanent. It is possible to change and be better. This is a crucial part of the journey towards authenticity.

Figure 5.4 – Changing our mindset

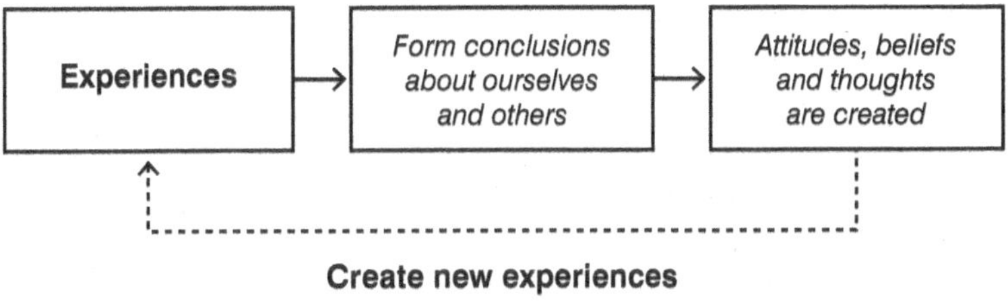

Whether it be a change of allowing others to speak first when you were previously the first to speak, asking more questions, giving or receiving feedback – when it is done in a deep acting way – it can become more natural than your previous behaviours.

Step 5: Develop capability

Early in my career as a leadership coach, I focused very heavily on what was a 'pure coaching' approach. This involved helping people to discover things for themselves and find their own solutions to problems they described to me in our coaching sessions. Even when I was met with *'I don't know'* I would stick to what I felt was the core of coaching principles and facilitated self-discovery through open questioning, probing and challenging.

However, a real awakening for me was when a leader, at the height of her understandable frustration with the process, said: *'But Allison, <u>how</u> do I coach people? And <u>how</u> do I delegate so that I can trust people? <u>How</u> do I give feedback in the best way? Do you have a model, a framework? Why keep asking me questions when I just don't know the answer? Can't you just tell me what to do?'*

She had a point. Sometimes, the only remaining barrier in translating intent to impact is precisely those practical skills. What I have come to realise is that there is a practical element to authenticity. There is a role alongside coaching, for tools, skills and methods to enable people to be *skilfully* authentic in carrying out their intent. It is the key reason I built directive leadership training into my leadership consulting business. Sometimes leaders want solutions not just questions!

In asking directly for answers, this particular leader was showing authenticity in her honest appraisal of herself and her need to develop skills. Indeed, a crucial part of acknowledging our imperfections and limitations is recognising that we must continually learn new skills. We can't be expected to know what these are all the time.

Learning skills is a critical adjunct to self-awareness, emotional intelligence, behavioural change and mindset shifts – and not just learning them, but embedding them, to the point of what is often referred to by trainers and facilitators as 'unconscious competence'[6] (see Figure 5.5).

Figure 5.5 – The unconscious competence cycle[7]

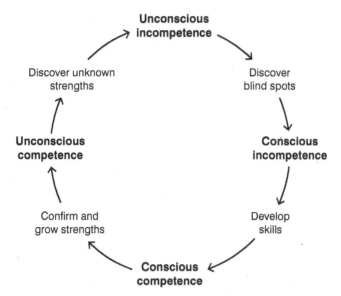

Note: Some articles and Wikipedia have stated that this model was first developed and featured by Martin M. Broadwell in 1969. The traditional model presents as a hierarchy or 'stages' of learning. In this adaptation, I have presented it as a cycle to represent continual life-long learning. I have also included what I believe to be the interim steps (or characteristics) of each stage that reflect concepts of self-awareness (through the discovery of blind spots), strengths awareness and strengths development.

It's true of course that when we are provided with new tools or techniques it can feel a little 'clunky'. For example, if you are moving from being directive as a leader to adopting a more coaching style, it feels odd and unnatural to be asking so many questions. That is when leaders tend to abandon what they learn and revert to more comfortable ways. It's critical to stay the course. The only way you can become comfortable and natural – and authentically skilful – is to practise and practise. Practise to the point of unconscious competence, where the new skills *become* natural and embed themselves in your leadership style as the new normal.

Step 6: Be discerning and adaptable

Being authentic doesn't necessarily mean that you can stop self-monitoring. It isn't enough to think that authenticity allows you (or others) a free pass. Authenticity also requires you to make conscious decisions about sharing and be discerning about vulnerability.

Best-selling author and researcher Brené Brown has written extensively and beautifully about embracing vulnerability, imperfection and revealing our true selves in her best-selling books *Daring Greatly*[8] and *The Gifts of Imperfection*.[9] It is certainly true that much more could be done to create environments where revealing our true selves is embraced and the strength in vulnerability is recognised.

More recently, Brown has responded[10] to the ever-growing conversation about what authenticity actually is and concerns that there is such a thing as 'too much' authenticity – through over sharing or speaking one's mind, no matter what we are thinking.

Brown writes that *'at the core of authenticity is the courage to be imperfect, vulnerable, and to set boundaries'*. Further, that *'real authenticity actually requires major self-monitoring and isn't the lack of self-monitoring. In fact, setting boundaries is, by definition, self-monitoring – it's thinking about what you're sharing, why you're sharing it, and with whom you should be sharing it.'*

That is, we must sometimes pause and discern whether it is the right place, right time, right audience and right context. This doesn't, however, discount the benefits in taking the risk of being vulnerable – a risk we often don't take.

Authenticity isn't simply about unfiltered communication. Some leaders may also think that authenticity is little more than being blunt and direct. The explanation they provide is typically along the lines of *'That's just me, I'm dead straight'*. However, unfiltered honesty that doesn't take account of the impact it is likely to have on the receiver can cause serious harm. Truly authentic leaders recognise the need to consider the likely impact of their response and actions (on themselves and others) before they speak or act. They consider if what they are about to do or say is aligned with their *desired* impact and intent for the people they are communicating with.

Step 7: Be a role model

People look to leaders and to their leadership style to get a sense of what is expected of them. In this way, being a role model of authenticity gains respect, as well as being an example for others to follow.

When I work with senior leaders and CEOs to facilitate 360-degree feedback, there is frequently what I refer to as an awakening. The sound of pennies dropping is almost audible as the reasons for leadership challenges are discovered and uncovered. What was once obvious frustration is replaced with excitement about new possibilities that are available from the knowledge they have gained.

At times, these leaders want to move quickly to implement the same process at the next level of the organisation and they often ask me to undertake a similar process with their staff. While this enthusiasm is both commendable and infectious, I have come to learn the risks of moving too quickly.

The issue is subtle, but it is found in the fact that once the next level of leadership, and the one after, and the one after that, undergo a similar process, these people will look up to their leaders above them to see evidence of embedded change. Embedded change – authentic change – requires effort, discipline and commitment. It is not a flash in the pan, Road to Damascus and then return-to-type experience. In fact, short-term change that is quickly lost in the daily pressure cooker of KPIs and targets, is a recipe for disaster and produces cynicism and a loss of faith and trust in the change as an authentic process.

Embed change by sharing

One way to embed change is for a leader to share the results of their feedback or coaching sessions with the team. In fact, one of the most authentic acts I've ever witnessed was a leader sharing his leadership feedback survey results with the entire organisation. This was no minor act. His results showed clear and strong feedback that employees were deeply dissatisfied with how he was leading.

He then publicly invited specific feedback, he actively listened, acknowledged the impact it was having and made specific and realistic commitments to change what he knew he could deliver on, along with a discussion on how his team could hold him accountable.

This took courage and guts, and it illustrated a real desire to make lasting change. For this specific leader, it was a powerful moment that is still talked about to this day. He let go of the need to be seen as perfect, accepted his impact and was a role model for the next level of leadership. This type of action is incredibly brave – and can have incredible impact. Despite some of us having a fear of not being approved of and not being seen as perfect, it can actually serve to raise the level of approval of us as leaders and allow for greater acceptance of some of our faults. It can lead to acceptance that we are not perfect and can allow patience for the fact that change might take some time. In my experience, people are more likely to approve of us when we let go of the need for approval!

Authenticity requires courage and it relies on us accepting that we must set an example to others. Ultimately, as leaders, we must be prepared to do ourselves what we expect others to do. This requires vulnerability, disclosure and a commitment to change.

Step 8: Feel and accept discomfort

Perhaps the most common misconception about authenticity is that it must feel 'comfortable' and 'natural'. Surely if we are showing our real selves, our vulnerabilities and our warts and all, we should find the whole thing a piece of cake!

The reality is that we often need to experience discomfort to be authentic. This is because if we have spent much of lives as leaders never being challenged, rarely reflecting and mostly feeling comfortable, we have likely been ignoring situations that will inevitably arise to test our values, intent and emotional reactions. The thing is, the more we sit in the discomfort, adjust ourselves and apply new skills, the less energy it takes and the more natural it becomes.

THE DARK SIDE OF AUTHENTICITY

The seemingly inexorable rise of political leaders such as Donald Trump and other independent politicians has raised some vexed questions about authenticity. A simple Google search of the words "Trump" and 'authentic' reveals a long list of articles and opinions on the topic: from CNN[11], *Forbes Magazine*[12], *The Financial Times*[13], to *The Australian*[14] along with many other blogs, research projects[15], surveys and thought pieces. The conversation is ongoing.

After the US Presidential Election in 2016, I sought to understand the perspectives of those who voted for Trump. Documentaries, traditional and social media commentary revealed a key aspect to the thinking among some voters, which could be summarised as: *'At least he says what he thinks!'*.

What was even more interesting was that some people valued his willingness to speak his mind, even if they didn't *agree* with his views. They were prepared to vote for someone who was transparent and real, regardless of their agreement with them.

Politics in Australia is following a similar trend. Independents and small parties are gaining votes from the 'traditional base' of the major parties. We tire of the career politician delivering the same talking points, scripted language and staying 'on message'. They are willing to trade off their beliefs and convictions and contradict themselves if there's a chance it will take down their opponents. If someone shows up who is willing to talk off-script and unfiltered, it's a refreshing change – a welcome disruption to the system.

What this amounts to is potentially both a protest against the apparent paucity of authenticity among career politicians and a willingness to reward as few as *two* aspects of authenticity – transparency and honesty – while turning a blind eye to other more troubling aspects of someone's leadership style and authenticity.

AUTHENTICITY – IT'S THE LONG GAME

The issue here is that true authenticity is a long game. It's a pattern of behaviour that is evidenced over time and over numerous examples and challenges. It involves more than just honesty and transparency. It seems to me to be no coincidence that many of these new-style politicians and the small parties they represent are mostly single or dual term. Or, once in a position of power they swap and change allegiance and even parties. Short-termism appears to be the order of the day.

Eventually, however, we tend to assess authenticity not just on someone's ability to say what they think, but on *what* they actually think, what they do, how they behave, their impact and how all of this relates to the results they achieve. Saying what you think might get you elected, but it's likely to lead to trouble down the track when the complex reality of actually leading hits home.

So, I view the dark side of authenticity as our tendency to view authentic leadership as being one-dimensional. Someone simply speaking their mind can be viewed as being authentic without considering the other factors that create a truly long-term, authentic impact.

Without greater authenticity across the political and party systems, independent politicians will continue to find themselves in the revolving door out of the corridors of power and the major parties will continue to watch their bases diminish. It will be disruption in the pursuit of authenticity, without actually achieving it.

THE RECENT EMERGENCE OF THE 'AUTHENTIC ORGANISATION'

'There are simply no shortcuts to creating long-term shareholder value'

—Bill George[16]

So far in this chapter we have looked at authenticity purely as an attribute that is applicable to individuals. While this is undoubtedly what this book is focused on, it would be remiss to leave the topic without at least a passing mention of one of the most interesting trends in business and leadership: the rise of the authentic organisation.

Social media, the access to immediate information and the ever-shortening news cycle are just some of the recent trends that have caused businesses and corporations to seek to benefit from the increasing emphasis on authenticity. Corporate values, visions and missions have migrated from the four walls of the boardroom to the Facebook newsfeeds, Instagram pages and LinkedIn discussion groups of many multinational, national and local businesses. These new media channels are littered with inspiring visions that provide aspiration and direction and ever-more purposeful mission statements that point to the heart of the impact an organisation hopes to have on customers and on the broader community. Corporate vision, mission and purpose has gone truly social.

When I am engaged by businesses to facilitate cultural change, invariably it comes down to one or both of two key objectives: sustainability and growth. Both are inherently long term. However, when all eyes are on profitability and shareholder value and the stresses that can come from financial pressure, decisions can be made to deliver short-term value. They can bypass or pay insufficient attention to the factors that actually 'create' those outcomes (see Figure 5.6).

Figure 5.6 – Alignment to create the authentic organisation

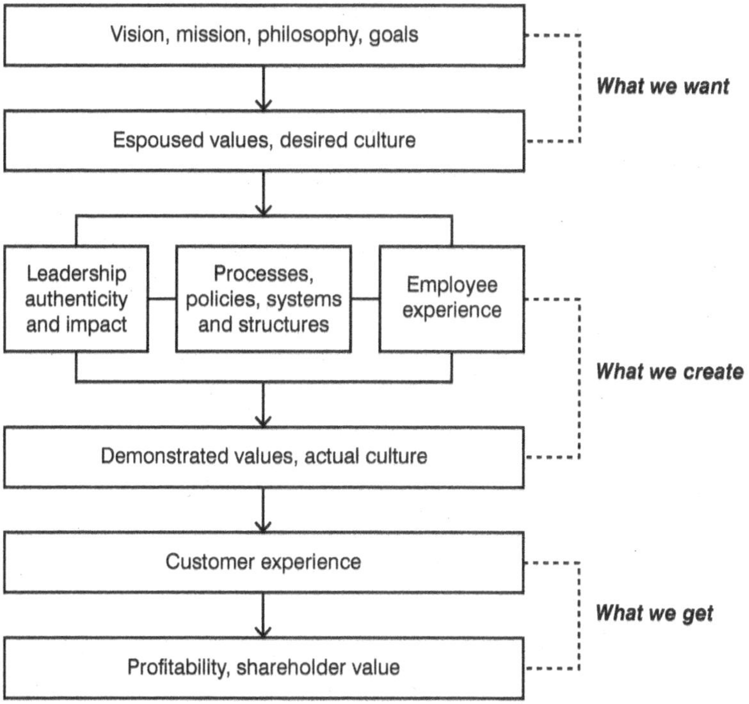

The result is incongruence and misalignment. The customer experience is vastly different to what was intended, and this can lead to eroding sustainability and growth, rather than building it. The customer experience comes *before* profitability and shareholder value, and there are many factors that create it. Taking shortcuts can fail to deliver long-term value, can erode reputation and trust and can make those now very public mission statements and values seem like little more than empty platitudes.

There are many examples that serve to demonstrate this.

The Australian Banking Royal Commission

The ongoing enquiry into Australia's banking sector has revealed some shocking practices in the financial advice industry. Advice that was meant to secure and build financial wealth for customers, ruined it. Decisions that benefited the adviser, the institution and the shareholder in the short term led to a devastating cost to customers. The result is that the level of trust in the financial advice sector is exceptionally low. The reputation of people in that sector has been tarnished, even among those advisers who conduct themselves ethically. The impacts are felt broadly and work to rebuild trust will be extensive.

Woolworths and its ownership of ALH Group

Australian supermarket giant Woolworths – *the fresh food people* – projects a wholesome, family-friendly image. Their television advertising slogan *'we understand what families go through'* illustrates where it sees itself in the lives, kitchens and dining rooms of families. Yet, Woolworths' significant share in the ALH Group, the owner and operator of around 12,000 poker machines with annual revenues in excess of $1.5 billion, has become something of a reputational thorn in the side for the iconic company. The issue of gambling-related losses and the often crippling and irreparable damage these can have on families that shows itself in relationship breakdown, physical and mental health issues and of course significant financial stress is beginning to become an issue that strikes at the authentic heart of Woolworths.

This apparent conflict between the image that Woolworths strives hard to project and the realities of its balance sheet has been acknowledged, to some extent, by the board. Woolworths' Chair, Gordon Cairns, responding to allegations that ALH had been involved in activities that encouraged gambling through the use of personal data and even 'spying' on people using poker machines, said, *If the allegations are true, then we have let ourselves down*. Indeed, he went even further and suggested that the future ownership of ALH by Woolworths was not guaranteed.

It's going to be interesting to watch how this situation unfolds in the coming months and years. What seems clear is that the public awareness of the damage caused to families is only going to increase. How will Woolworths – and others – react? Will they continue to invest in an area of their business that, while immensely profitable, appears to risk the organisational authenticity of a business that relies in large part on public trust, consumer loyalty and a family-friendly image? What seems to be very clear is that the public can turn very quickly against companies that appear to say one thing and yet do another.

The #metoo movement and its impact on longstanding HR practice

In the wake of revelations about Hollywood director Harvey Weinstein, the #metoo movement was born, exposing widespread experiences of sexual harassment and misconduct in the work-place. This has sparked another conversation about authentic organisations. Organisations have been exposed as taking a 'risk management' approach to protect themselves, rather than protecting those experiencing harm. 'Zero tolerance' policies are also questionable alongside 'mediation' practices. Punishment of complainants, protection of perpetrators, payouts and non-disclosure agreements have made the bowels of unpleasant HR practices a matter for public discussion. Questions are now being raised about the ethics of such practices and the legal validity. All of these things demonstrate a willingness to trade off organisational values and the wellbeing of people.

Authenticity is increasingly being questioned and people are demanding more information and transparency about what organisations do and how they do it. Employees are breaking silences. What was previously an underbelly of organisational culture is being flipped and exposed. Transparency is the new currency of the authentic organisation.

Authentic organisations monitor and guard what they 'create' and align it with their intent, with the same level of rigour and tenacity as financial results. Rather than investing energy on 'recovery' (of reputation, share price, customer trust), authentic organisations spend energy on alignment with the intent and mission, through:

1. Leadership impact
2. Processes, policies, systems and structures
3. The employee experience
4. Actual values and culture.

Not only must these factors be aligned, they must be monitored and measured. Measures of 'employee engagement' and 'customer satisfaction' are not enough. They need to be supplemented with feedback and measurement on authenticity.

THE FINAL WORD ON AUTHENTICITY

- The modern workforce is less like to 'follow' a leader, but rather align itself to people who are authentic and whom they trust and believe.
- Authenticity is more than being yourself. It is about creating a connection between intent and impact (through alignment of mindset, behaviours and skills). It often requires change.
- The personal cost of being inauthentic is facing judgement, making trade-offs and a waste of energy.
- Common barriers to authenticity are: adopting a persona, seeking approval, being in control, striving for perfection, making comparisons to others, avoiding discomfort, compliance and conformity, capability and unconscious beliefs, attitudes and behaviours.
- Creating alignment requires self-awareness, emotional intelligence and changing behaviour.
- Alignment involves crafting your intent (purpose, mission, values and impact), sharing your intent, seeking feedback, self-reflection, adjusting behaviour, developing capability, being discerning and adaptable, being a role model for others and accepting discomfort.
- The rise of the authentic organisation also requires alignment between the mission and espoused values and the customer experience.

- Authentic organisations create alignment through leadership impact, processes, systems, policies, structures, the employee experience and culture.
- Measurement of organisational authenticity involves measuring the factors that create alignment.

Acknowledgement

While I'm a self-confessed professional and personal development junkie, and continually learning and researching, I'd like to acknowledge the influence that the work of Human Synergistics International has had on my thinking, knowledge and experience over many years. Their commitment to rigorous research, evidence-based measurement of culture and leadership impact, has been a key factor in me forming keen insights and achieving transformational change in both my own development and work with clients.

IN CONVERSATION

Interviews with five leaders who lead well

Having been a Member of the Institute of Managers and Leaders, Australia and New Zealand since I was a student at the University of New South Wales and having the honour of being elected Chair of the Board of Directors in 2014, I have so many fond memories and highlights of my time at AIM and now IML.

However, nothing comes close to the time I have spent meeting with, talking to and networking with my fellow Members and the other non-Member managers and leaders. Over these 30 years, I have learnt so much about leadership, about how to lead well and about the essence of sound management practice from these remarkable women and men. It's also true to say that my own journey of discovery and development about leadership continues at every IML event, Masterclass, Conference, TEL Talk and networking evening that I attend today.

Listening to and learning from the experiences of others is an immensely important part of the journey that is leadership. I know that I owe much of my own approach to leadership and my management style to the stories and anecdotes that I have heard from others along the way.

As part of this book we decided to continue the IML tradition of talking to leaders about the way they lead and about their personal approach to the seven attributes of successful leadership covered in this book.

Each interview offers a unique insight into the lives of leaders in a particular field – from sport to business to academia to not-for-profit. I find that it is often from these types of personal insights that we can develop our own leadership strategies and techniques. I know that I left each interview with these five leaders resolving to implement something different in my own leadership life. I hope you do too.

I hope you find these conversations with five leaders about leading well as revealing and as practical as I did!

Ann Messenger FIML
Chair, Institute of Managers and Leaders, Australia and
New Zealand

Georgie Harman

Chief Executive, beyondblue

Why do you think it is important for leaders to show integrity?

Integrity is fundamental to strong, effective leadership because it is tied closely to trust. Trust and credibility are the new capital of leadership and people are placing more and more store in them in deciding who they want to work with and for. Most people are pretty clued in – they will know when you are being true to yourself and your values, and they know when you are not. As a leader, your values and moral compass are on display with every interaction, every decision you make. If leaders expect integrity from their employees, their employees are right to expect the same in return.

Give an example of how you demonstrate integrity in your role.

At beyondblue, we know how powerful personal experience and storytelling is in educating others, challenging thinking, changing behaviour and smashing stigma. Every day we ask people who live with or who have experienced a mental health issue to share their insights with us and with the community. To me, integrity means walking the talk. I have opened up publicly about the mental health challenges I've faced and how I dealt with them. Sharing my story has strengthened my resolve, changed my views about what a 'strong' leader is, and shown my team that I need them too.

Leaders were once expected to be emotionally detached – this is now changing. Why do you think that good leadership involves being in tune with the emotions of the people you lead?

The ability to be strong, take decisive calls, stand by those decisions and accept when they weren't the best, take the rap and hold yourself accountable are all traditional leadership qualities. What isn't commonly spoken about when it comes to leadership is human connection, vulnerability and accessibility. The 'school of leadership' teaches us hard skills but knowing who you are as a person is fundamental to your ability to lead well. More and more, people want to work in environments, and with people, who are genuine. Knowing yourself helps you understand and manage your own behaviour and relationships. In many ways, this is the essence of good leadership.

Today's leaders tend to be incredibly busy with numerous, often conflicting, priorities; what do you do to ensure that you are aware of the emotions of your immediate team?

Our leadership team has worked hard to build trust and I hope that means we've together built a culture where we all look out for and notice changes in each other and don't ignore them. The busier I am, the more blinkered and direct I can be, but I'm confident my team will call me out and let me know if they need my time for something important. I try to reflect on my own demeanour and interactions after a particularly busy spell and check back in if I think I need to. When I sense I need to, I check in – either on-on-one or as a group. I'm not sure I do this enough.

Authenticity is one of the most common terms used when discussing leadership today. What do you see as being at the heart of the term 'Authentic Leadership'?

This idea of authentic leadership has become something of a buzzword; in fact, I'm starting to become a bit irritated by it! That's problematic because it's a quality I have a deep personal and professional belief in. To me it means not trying to be something you're not. I've come on a journey in this myself. I've come to the view that I can't be anything other than my whole self. I've realised that you don't need to change yourself as you become a leader, you just need to be yourself and that means being vulnerable sometimes.

I once thought being a strong, authentic leader meant I was the one who charged to the front, took the bullet, had all the answers and was the most resilient. But what you really need is to build a team you can rely on and trust. You still lead, take the tough decisions, but you do so knowing your team has your back, just as you have theirs.

How do you show 'the real you' at work? What practical tips do you have for people?

Open communication and face-to-face contact are basic principles – and it's not the big, grandiose statements or the inspiring speeches, it's the hundred small things. Smiling, saying good morning, walking the long way around the floor rather than the shortcut to your desk. I like the people I work with and I'm interested in understanding what makes them tick.

Let people understand who you really are; what your values system is. Then, when you have to take hard decisions, such as changing the business or making people redundant, you have a reference point. Allowing people to see your vulnerabilities helps them understand you're human, just like them.

I've talked openly to senior leaders and thousands of others about circumstances that have impacted my own mental health and wellbeing, and my ability to manage the life events that hit all of us from time to time; how they impact us personally as well as professionally. There is a fine line, of course, between sharing and sharing too much! You have to find that balance.

What practical steps do you take to ensure that you know your own strengths, weaknesses, blind spots and development areas?

It's important to stay curious, to seek out further insights and opportunities to grow personally and professionally. Wherever possible, I tune in for feedback from mentors, friends and colleagues. Building trust in your team is vital, as is knowing how to listen without being defensive. Feedback enhances self-awareness and empathy, and helps you understand how your actions affect others. You also need to identify your pressure points and what unblocks them. What causes you to feel stressed? What relaxes you? These also happen to be some of the basics of keeping your mental health on track, so it's not only leaders who can benefit from these ideas. We are just as likely to be the one in five of all Australians who will experience a mental health issue this year.

Self-awareness is sometimes viewed as challenging – even threatening – as it often involves gathering feedback and changing. Can you give an example of a change to your leadership style following feedback?

I take advice from my executive team about my own performance, and a consistent theme for me has been delegation and letting go. I need to do more of it, more often. I've had to learn to focus on fewer tasks more intently, more mindfully.

A US study, The CEO Genome project, examined the characteristics of an effective CEO. The findings were quite different from what boards usually consider. The traditional thinking is that a CEO should be strong and charismatic – someone who can hold the room's attention, maintain and improve shareholder confidence, back their own judgement and inspire others. But this research found consistency and reliability – characteristics often thought a little mundane – were more important. Delegation certainly helps on these points.

John Buchanan

**Coach of the Australian Cricket Team (1999–2007),
Leadership and Business Consultant**

Why do you think it is important for leaders to show integrity?

Leaders can only lead if they have followers. Followers will only follow if they have faith, respect and belief in the leader. Faith, respect and belief will only come from a leader doing what he or she says they will do – consistently and to the standards they expect of others.

Give an example of how you demonstrate integrity in your role.

The first step is to clearly understand your leadership or coaching philosophy – your values, principles, cornerstones. It is these that a leader does not compromise; otherwise, they will be seen to be a person of questionable integrity.

One of my cornerstones is to develop a relationship with the 'whole person' – not simply the athlete or the staff member. I would like to be able to know as much about a person as they choose to let me know. I will also get to know more about the individual through peers, friends and family.

In this way, I believe I can be far more helpful to them, if I understand as much about the person as possible.

Leaders were once expected to be emotionally detached – this is now changing. Why do you think that good leadership involves being in tune with the emotions of the people you lead?

Leadership at its simplest level is about relationships. Relationships are built on many levels, one of which is about being in touch with the emotional drivers of an individual – what makes them afraid, anxious, excited, happy, withdrawn, angry, etc.

So by trying to understand the 'whole person', I can as a leader be in a better position to know when to be the leader, the coach, the parent, the guide, the disciplinarian, the psychologist, the friend, the conscience and so on.

Today's leaders tend to be incredibly busy with numerous, often conflicting, priorities; what do you do to ensure that you are aware of the emotions of your immediate team?

Good leaders will spend time with their people, or at least their immediate reach of most influence. Good leaders will also spend time observing how individuals react in different circumstances. Good leaders will engage in regular feedback – both informal and formal – to ensure that what they are observing or seeing is accurate both in delivery and why it is being delivered in a particular way.

What do you do in your role to inspire your team?

People are naturally competitive – either bettering themselves or trying to beat others.

The leader's job is to constantly set challenges for individuals and collectively for the group or the team – to take the individual and the team outside their comfort zones.

In being challenged, the individuals and the team need to know that there is a degree of 'safety'; that is to say, it is a learning environment in which things can go wrong due to being stretched beyond existing technical, physical, mental and tactical limits.

So, when things go right or wrong, the leader is encouraging of the learnings to be taken, more so than the outcome produced.

Who inspires you and why?

What inspired me recently was an interview by Channel 7's Pat Welsh with Kurt Fearnley, right at the conclusion of Kurt's marathon win at the Gold Coast Commonwealth Games. It was an inspiring physical achievement in its own right. But what was really inspiring was the four-minute interview where Kurt spoke to what put him in that situation.

With exhaustion obvious, he spoke of the incredible regime of training that put him in a position to win. He spoke of the pain in the race, but he suffered the pain as a small measure of what he could give back to all those who have supported him for so long – incredible determination, and a will, to not give up.

He captured this in a word – FIERCE. He was fierce on course today. He then spoke to not being able to do it alone, or indeed be alone. He captured this in a word – KINDNESS.

He encouraged all young people (and for him there is no distinction between able body or not) to show kindness to all those around them: their supporters, family, friends, competitors. And finally, he wrapped it up with FAMILY. 'Do not leave them behind', he said. 'Bring them with you on the journey. They are the ones who truly know you, the joys and sorrows, the sacrifices and the achievements – they are the ones who love you no matter what'.

Authenticity is one of the most common terms used when discussing leadership today. What do you see as being at the heart of the term 'Authentic Leadership'?

Authentic leadership flows from completely understanding yourself as a leader and delivering that every moment of every day. And when you cannot do that for whatever reason, inside your control or outside, the authentic leader will take full responsibility and be accountable for their actions and behaviours.

What practical steps do you take to ensure that you know your own strengths, weaknesses, blind spots and development areas?

Where I had the opportunity to hire assistants, I did not want to hire John Buchanan 'look-a-likes'. I wanted people with different backgrounds, ideas and methods. I did want to know that we shared similar philosophies. Difference meant I would be challenged by the people around me – which was healthy for me and for them.

Respect is an underrated attribute for leaders. Do you think it's important for leaders to show respect – and why is this?

Respect should be shown by everyone – formal leader or not. However, respect may initially be accorded to an individual or a group by way of their formal title, a ranking. It may also be accorded by outcomes achieved, results and performance.

Real respect though is earned by the consistency of one's actions and behaviours – through integrity and through authenticity already mentioned. Because bound up in these words are values such as trust, honesty, transparency, accountability.

Hannah Critchlow

Neuroscientist, Science Outreach Fellow, Magdalene College, Cambridge University

Leaders were once expected to be emotionally detached – this is now changing. Why do you think that good leadership involves being in tune with the emotions of the people you lead?

The myriad emotions that we each experience help to shape our unique reality and affect how we each react to, and interact with, the world.

Emotions have been crucial for our survival, acting as strong driving forces behind the evolution of our basic behaviours. Feelings of pleasure, for example, helped motivate our ancestors to expend the necessary energy in order to obtain food, water and to reproduce. Feelings of fear and disgust helped us to steer clear of potentially hazardous situations. And as scientists explore emotions, in the context of the current revolution in technologies available to research, they are revealing the precise mechanisms within the brain that enable such strong emotive associations to be passed down across generations. The results help support the age-old concept that emotions are strong signals that should be listened to, and reflected upon, on both a species-wide and individual basis, that they are an important aspect of our ability to learn, remember and to put it simply, be the subjective, fully conscious beings that we are.

But why exactly are emotions necessary? If we think of emotions as the end result of information processing without our conscious awareness, surely this begs the question that our brain should be sophisticated enough to possess the ability to process information from the outside world and rationally decipher it without emotions colouring our decisions? Unfortunately not, and the reason for this is due to the energy demands and limited power potential of the brain.

Our brains are exceptionally busy places: containing over 86 billion nerve cells, each connected to up to 10,000 others busy sending electrical and chemical signals zipping along the circuit board that make up our mind. This tangle of cells, our brain's complex connectome, has to process vast amounts of information coming in from the outside world, make sense of it all, put it into context based on our prior experience, and then instruct our bodies how to react to our ever-changing external reality. The brain is a mesmerising dynamic and fascinating beast, consuming just over 20% of our daily energy quota in order to accomplish this majestic feat. But in order for our brains, our minds, to operate at such a consistently high speed, it has to take shortcuts in information-processing, make assumptions based on prior experiences. Much of this occurs without our conscious awareness.

Occasionally our brains need to highlight specific aspects of this unconscious processing. It's thought that emotional cues are employed in order to do this by tagging or emphasising specific past associations with defined neurochemical signature responses (e.g. the feelings of happiness, anxiety, joy, fear, competitiveness). Such feelings help us to respond accordingly; using our unconscious processing they match the current situation with past experiences and their outcome and assign it an emotion, without wasting any additional information that would be necessary to piece together all of the new incoming information and consciously make sense of it. If we view emotions in this light, we see that they are helpful, efficient brain cues that should be listened to on both an individual and a group level.

It is important to add a note of caution to this emotional tale: there are times, unfortunately, when emotions can escalate and amplify. Perhaps a seemingly irrational fear or an obsessive or intrusive paranoid thought might arise, which can be difficult to dislodge and get in the way of important decision-making. In this case it is possible that past experiences can cloud judgements in a negative way. Tips on how to help prevent this situation from occurring are discussed in the question below.

In general, however, emotions are largely important brain processes that it is wise to listen to, reflect upon, and act with their being in mind. In previous times an ethos prevailed, particularly in the domain of leadership and management, instructing emotional detachment, that true strength relied on one's ability to make cold, calculated, decisions, without the taint of emotional response. However, as we start to understand more about the neurobiology of emotions, this view is changing with emphasis shifting on listening to not just our own emotions, but those of others within the team.

Today's leaders tend to be incredibly busy with numerous, often conflicting, priorities; what do you do to ensure that you are aware of the emotions of your immediate team?

As we discover more about how the brain operates and how emotions are forged we are reminded that good leadership involves being in tune with not only the emotions of yourself but also of those people that you lead. In order to gain the most from team members it is important that their opinions, past experiences and emotional responses to scenarios are listened to and discussed, that they feel their experience and expertise, both at the conscious and unconscious level, is valued.

There is robust scientific research on how to employ emotions wisely in our work and life decisions. The data aligns with the following ancient, and intuitively common sense, practices that collectively help to create an environment that facilitates and cultivates not a knee-jerk emotional response but one of deeper emotional intelligence:

- Ability to openly communicate without fear
- Practising the art of self-reflection
- Exercise.

These three practices help to provide the necessary foundations that enable us to develop a more flexible approach in the future. This all helps to ensure that we keep learning, and so make new emotional responses, rather than getting bogged down by past emotional baggage. In this way emotions can be used for pro-active and positive decision-making both at work and at home.

What do you do in your role to inspire your team?

Luckily, I am naturally a glass-half-full, positive kind of person! Also, with my strategic work head on, enthusiasm and passion can be positively contagious behaviours, so it makes sense to exude as much of these characteristics as possible with your team mates – in the hope they will rub off on them and help them get the job done more efficiently and productively.

Previously I've set up a lunchtime running group to help enthuse colleagues and keep their spirits up during the dark UK winter months. For staff who have expressed anxiety over specific projects/events I work closely with them to ensure they are prepared and happy with each aspect of the itinerary and that they feel confident discussing issues for me.

Wherever possible I try to emphasise to colleagues that life, both in work and out, is an experience-gathering and problem-solving exercise, that we each have different strengths and idiosyncrasies but by working collectively almost anything can be solved! For some, who I think need an extra confidence boost, I've been known to get them to join me for an entertaining power dance, stretching all the limbs and assuming strong stances immediately before they go live with the project/give a talk/interview.

I also take time to clearly articulate my thought processes behind important decisions and emphasise why particular jobs are so important to get right. I ask colleagues for their feedback, where appropriate, so that they feel valued (which helps to increase their work satisfaction and productively). This also has added benefit that their wisdom might help my decision-making to evolve so that a better solution is reached.

I try to inspire an ability to be aware of one's own limitations and work round them. For example, personally I can find it very difficult to focus on tasks in hand if there are any distractions. So, if there is a job that requires complete focus I will work from home, or in a quiet library, completely solo, and to a tight deadline, in order to complete it.

I make sure that team members and colleagues feel comfortable discussing their weaknesses and looking for clever strategies to help overcome or negate them. Also I encourage them to think creatively in order to help create an environment or situation that helps to get the best outcome for the project as a whole.

What practical steps do you take to ensure that you know your own strengths, weaknesses, blind spots and development areas?

I try to spend at least six hours a week exercising. Ideally by myself, either jogging (fairly slowly it has to be said!) or cycling down the towpaths in Cambridge and across the Fens or in whichever city or landscape I find myself travelling to. Moving seems to open my mind, giving me the time and space I need to reflect on what I have achieved, what I need to do next, and consider any emotional response I have more analytically, to try to understand why I feel the way I do. I also use this time to consider how I can improve situations for the future, thinking creatively about how to tackle and react to specific situations. I don't set out on these exercise jaunts thinking that I will focus on specific aspects of my life, I simply find my mind naturally wanders to these places and without exercise I generally start to get anxious and to ruminate in a negative way.

I've also tried yoga, meditation classes, aerobic exercise training, visiting the gym, etc., but generally these forms of inside prescriptive exercise don't really help raise my self-awareness at all. In fact, yoga and meditation generally stress me out to extent that I get cold sores after each class. (Perhaps there is an extra level of self-awareness down there that I am completely burrowing! Or I prefer to think that I need to be moving in the outside natural air with sunlight on me in order to think clearly!)

A second practical step I take is to try to ensure colleagues and wise friends feel comfortable providing me with honest, frank, constructive, feedback. I politely and explicitly ask for constructive criticism on my projects, emphasising how much I value and appreciate their insights, and that it could help me to help shape future work positively. I try to take the criticism on board without showing a negative or defensive reaction to it. I may not necessarily totally follow through with everyone else's advice: I may strongly disagree with their opinion, think they may be operating with their own biases in this case, or believe that the feedback is not relevant to the specific scenario. But I find it important to solicit, evaluate and be grateful for other people taking the time to let you know what they think!

Self-awareness is sometimes viewed as challenging – even threatening – as it often involves gathering feedback and changing. Can you give an example of a change to your leadership style following feedback?

Literally on a daily basis I do this! My insights from neuroscience have left me appreciating how incredibly sophisticated our brains are!

Ann Sherry

Chair, Carnival Cruises Australia

Why do you think it's important for leaders to show integrity?

It's important because you've got to stand for something. And these days if you stand for nothing then I think it's really hard to get people to follow you.

I think integrity is an interesting issue because in a world where business leaders have such poor reputations, standing for something, having integrity, being principled and not waxing and waning as the mood takes you, or the world pushes you, becomes even more important – people are looking for beacons of hope. Often inside organisations people are looking to their leadership for a reason to keep working there. Standing for something, being really clear about who you are and what you do and why you do it, which I guess would be my definition of integrity, is really fundamental.

What do you do to ensure that you're aware of the emotions of the people that you work with and particularly your immediate team?

I think there are two things. One is you've got to engage with people. I've always been a huge rap for open plan offices, if for no other reason than you're socially engaging with people as you move around. You're not locked in your own little cubicle space where you can avoid everybody. I think that was the hidey hole for people who didn't like communicating. You've got to be talking to people, asking them questions, being engaged with them socially and then you pick up very quickly on the mood, the feeling (is the mood positive, negative, anxious, optimistic, pessimistic? What's going on?) It allows you to interrogate as well. You can ask people what's going on.

My view on emotional intelligence generally is there are a lot of people who are not that interested. They may be so-called leaders, but they're not that interested in what's going on around them. They believe that they somehow are the font of all wisdom and knowledge. I think there's real threshold issue with emotional intelligence; you've got to understand or believe that it's important to ask people around you what they're doing and what they're thinking because it's the collective effort that will get you where you want to be as a business.

This is not a solo journey. It's like trekking across the North Pole by yourself – you wouldn't do it. Engaging, understanding, listening and questioning helps you engage with whomever, whatever and wherever you are, and being present when you are there. So, if I'm here I'm present here. Yesterday, I was at a board meeting, so my mind was on that environment, I was present there thinking about who the people were, what was going on, what did it look and feel like, because you've got to use your own radar as well.

What do you do in your role to inspire your team?

One thing is that I do what I say I'm going to do. Some inspiration is just being there, being present, doing what you say you're going to do and following through on stuff you promise. I'm a big believer also in setting aspirational objectives. I think you need to look three years out and say, 'Where could we be?' 'Imagine if...' So there's a piece of my style that's about taking us out further and maybe even setting targets that you may look at now and think, 'Oh God, how are we ever going to do that?'

One aspirational objective was my one million passengers! I committed publicly that we would have one million passengers cruising by 2020 at a time when that was unimaginable. So that was macro, and we do it at the micro level as well. Imagine if we were the first business to go into the Solomon Islands after all their difficult rebuilding of community and really work with the local community to create a tourism industry. Imagine what that would do in the Solomon Islands. And of course, we've done it. But those things become possible because you create a sense of possibility that helps give people a reason to want to come to work. It gives people a reason to think what they're doing has more meaning than whatever they're doing in their day jobs. It gives meaning and it gives context as well which is really important.

Who inspires you and why?

Anyone really who I think sees opportunity where everybody else sees either the status quo or obstacles. I've just done the judging of the 100 Women of Influence awards for this year with the *Australian Financial Review* and Qantas. There are only 10 categories, so there are 10 winners and then an overall winner.

There were so many astonishing stories of women young and old, country and city – who found themselves in very difficult personal circumstances and rather than just fix it for themselves, they fixed it for everybody else. Or they saw an opportunity to just do something really differently and chased it and raised the money or got the money to get whatever it took. For me, that's the hallmark of real leadership and that's the stuff that helps countries get better and communities get better.

Fortunately, I get to see these examples and so I am inspired by that. In terms of me, personally, as I've gone on my journey, there have been people who've backed me almost against the odds. I've always felt that I then had the obligation to really show up and make it work. I try to do that for other people because I've felt personally how empowering that is to have someone say, 'We'll put you in this job. We really want you to achieve something big and we think you can do it.'

What do you do at work to show the real you and what practical tips do you have for people around authenticity and showing their real selves at work?

It's an interesting question. The first thing I'd say about authenticity is the real test of authenticity is whether you behave differently in the outside world than you do at work. One of my famous stories is about my early days at Westpac, where a colleague used to roll up in the car park in a convertible, sleeves rolled up, loud music blaring. He would get into the car park, close the roof and roll his sleeves down. He'd drop in to this other person and then he'd go to work and would be boring, inaccessible, difficult to deal with. At the end of the day, you'd watch him get into his car back to his other self. It took someone to challenge him to bring his real self to work.

People who work in organisations see that a lot in their leadership. The ability to be the same person in and out of work I think fundamentally is what authenticity is about.

The second thing is to share bits of your personal self. You don't have to bring it all to work if you don't want to. But people do need to get a bit of a window on who you really are and who are the people around you.

So, we do very simple things sometimes like Bring Your Kids to Work Day. It might seem like a pretty naff idea but you watch the impact that something small like this has on the entire organisation. In teams you see other people's kids, you see the way they engage, you sort of feel like you get a bit closer to them. The other thing I like to do is, instead of taking everyone out to a restaurant for a staff do, I invite people to my home. I think there's something personal about opening your own environment, and letting people see you in your own environment, so they can see that you are the same there as you are at work. It's not an act here or an act there. You know, taking people into a domestic environment is personal.

I do this when people visit from overseas too, instead of going out for a meal with them I invite them to my home (it's often cheaper as well!). I'm not pretending that I cook for everyone, but it's nice to take people into a domestic environment and it feels more intimate, it feels as though people can talk with you. They see the chaos of your life – everyone's lives are messy. My son bounces in and says, 'Hi everyone!' and you know the way it works; the dogs sit under the table, you know that's the way it is!

What practical steps do you take to ensure that you know your own strengths and particularly weaknesses and blind spots?

For me there are a couple of things. Regular feedback is obviously part of that. It's interesting as often you watch your weaknesses hoping they get better and sometimes they do. But it's a good way of saying, 'I'm finding a blind spot'. I think in different circles, different businesses, different roles, your blind spots can change.

The second is through direct engagement with people. This allows you to build trust and for people to say stuff to you that they don't write. In fact, I had a conversation today and someone said to me, 'You know you sometimes send us all a bit crazy!' People engage with you more directly and do challenge you on your blind spots. So, sometimes it's actually just about good communication with the people around you and trust. They trust that you won't react when they raise issues with you, which is valuable as I think we all have blind spots.

The other thing for me is I do give people quite direct feedback, which I always think is good for them but not everybody receives it that way. So, one of my blind spots is that – and I have to consciously moderate this – I'm very direct and most people don't get very direct feedback ever. And so sometimes that comes across as harsher than I'm intending. It's one of the reasons I've got to be present when I'm doing those things – I see it, I process it, I tell you and I then watch you go, 'ugh!'. Then I think, oh my God, I shouldn't have done that! And then I've got to recover. It's one of those things that, again, some people say they love the fact that I give them such direct feedback but not everybody loves it.

How do you personally balance the power you have as a leader – I think the days of leaders denying power is over, we do have power – how do you balance that power with the respect that you show to those you lead?

One thing is not ever assuming I'm omnipotent. We were talking earlier about leaders who think they are somehow heroic individuals! That's not my style at all. I pay no homage to that model and in fact think it's nonsense and has been very damaging. So, for me leadership is, in fact, about continually testing that the people that you think you're leading are interested in what you're doing and saying, and therefore want to come along with you on the journey. So, the respect for me is testing that – even when I say outrageous things like we will have a million passengers – actually testing with people whether that can be a collective ambition. I listen to the anxiety this creates in some people. You can't just say it and then run away and hope everybody gets on with it. The respect piece comes from actually going back and revisiting and reprocessing and making sure that people are pulling in the same direction.

Do you have a strategy for sound decision-making and how do you create the right environment for yourself so that you can make the right decisions?

There are three things. Right decisions require good information. So, it's taking the time to get the information you think you need. The second is you need to find some quiet reflective time to process things, then maybe you need to come back, talk to people, before going back into decision-making mode. This is so you're making space and head space to think about things more clearly. Being decisive is about doing all those things. There will always be more than one outcome you can come up with. For me it's about picking it out, picking what you think is the right way forward given everything that you know and not retesting it too quickly because that creates ambiguity and indecision. If you do that, people around you know they need to wait a bit longer because you haven't really made the decision. So when I've made a decision, I'm clear that I have made a decision. If people want to challenge it then that's fine but challenge the decision from a fact base. Don't challenge it from an emotional point of view or because you don't believe it can happen.

I think making good decisions requires good information, requires clear head space to contemplate.

I sometimes say to people I make my best decisions after I've been out in the garden for a couple of hours, doing things that are very grounding, where you haven't got the white noise that sometimes you have at work that's just distracting. After a dog walk I am really clear on things because everything's clear. You can focus on something else. Going for a walk or even just sitting quietly and getting your brain to be still.

Meredith Staib FIML

**Chief Executive, Royal Flying Doctor Service
(Queensland Section)**

Why do you think it is important for leaders to show integrity?

Integrity is probably one of the most important traits for a leader to have. It is fundamental to building mutually respectful and trusting relationships. To me, integrity is about being fair, honest, consistent and open – then you will earn the trust of your people. I find the simplest approach is to treat people the way you would like to be treated yourself.

Give an example of how you demonstrate integrity in your role.

When I think about the primary role of the Royal Flying Doctor Service – assisting people in remote and regional Australia when they need it the most – I am reminded of how critical integrity is to the job we do. Our people must trust each other, work together, and stand by the values of the organisation. We work in a high-pressure environment where time, teamwork and trust are paramount to getting the right outcome.

I try to lead by example by being ethical and remaining true to my personal values.

A tip for anyone looking to take a new leadership position – make sure your values and the values of the organisation align before you take the role. It should be a key part of your decision-making process. If your values are compromised, you will find it very difficult to act authentically and with integrity.

Leaders were once expected to be emotionally detached – this is now changing. Why do you think that good leadership involves being in tune with the emotions of the people you lead?

Emotional intelligence is a key skill that all leaders should nurture and develop. While some people naturally have it spades, I do think it is something that can be cultivated and improved over time.

For me, high EI is more about listening than talking. It's about picking up on non-verbal cues, anticipating reactions by putting yourself in somebody else's shoes, and knowing what response will motivate your team or leave them feeling unempowered.

As the world of work continues to change rapidly and uncertainty becomes the norm, understanding how your employees are feeling and appreciating their differing responses to change will be key to knowing how to get the best out of them.

When you're in tune with your people, you can anticipate reactions and responses and you can also motivate by tapping into people's key drivers. But most importantly, it helps you treat people with respect, no matter what the conversation or decision.

Today's leaders tend to be incredibly busy with numerous, often conflicting, priorities; what do you do to ensure that you are aware of the emotions of your immediate team?

I have just started in a new organisation as CEO, so the most important first step for me was to get to know the people. In this new role, my goal was to establish an open, honest and frank relationship with the people in my team so that I'm aware of their individual strengths and weaknesses and the type of environment they need to perform at their best. Equally, this 'getting to know you' period helps my team understand more about me – my values, my goals for the organisation, and the role they can play in helping to achieve this.

When you have a good relationship with your team, they will tell you their honest thoughts, which is invaluable in making the right decisions to drive an organisation forward.

I also think that celebrating success is important. Not just at the end of a long project or organisational milestone, but along the way.

My advice is to spend the time with your people.

What do you do in your role to inspire your team?

The most important thing you can do is unite your team around the vision of your organisation. If people are clear about the organisation's goals and its direction it will give them a sense of purpose. People must be able to see themselves in the vision, so find out what motivates your people, then give them the opportunity to follow their motivations. Don't be afraid to adjust roles or add in elements that play to a person's strengths. Make sure their efforts are always aligned to the vision. That way they know their contribution is important.

Be open to new ideas. Empowering people to think for themselves and solve problems creatively is the greatest way to encourage your team to build a future for themselves and the organisation.

I also think leading by example and remaining highly visible is important; leaders must lead from the front and serve from the back, this way people will feel both inspired and supported.

Also, make sure you have some fun along the way.

Who inspires you and why?

I'm fortunate to have worked for, and with, some great leaders. I think it is important that you take every opportunity to learn something from them all.

You should build or develop your own unique style as a leader; you need to be your own version of yourself. I have learnt from amazing nursing leaders, business executives and from my peers.

I have also been a mentor myself and would hope to continue to do this during my career. I feel that it is my responsibility to give back to the profession I work in, and particularly to other women.

How do you show 'the real you' at work and what practical tips do you have for people?

People are good at spotting fakes, so my advice is to be your authentic self. When your personal values align well with the values of the organisation it's not difficult to be 'the real you' as it will come naturally. That said, there are things you can do to make sure you're acting naturally, with honesty and with integrity.

Always ensure your emotional intelligence is 'fully tuned'. This is essentially about listening and observing. You also need to be humble enough to ask for help or to seek out different viewpoints to make sure your mind is open, and you're not swayed by personal bias or habit.

What practical steps do you take to ensure that you know your own strengths, weaknesses, blind spots and development areas?

It is important to be authentic and honest in your dealings with people. I have learnt a great deal from the people around me, so I make a point of asking for feedback, opinions and for help when I need it. I often gain great insight into my own strengths and weaknesses during this process, which is invaluable.

More formally, when I was onboarded as CEO, the management team and I all completed a DiSC profile so that we understood each other's workplace priorities, motivators, stressors and style. This meant we could make the most of our differences to improve the effectiveness of each team.

Respect is an underrated attribute for leaders. Do you think it's important for leaders to show respect – and why is this?

As with integrity, respect is a cornerstone of effective leadership. Integrity and respect go hand-in-hand, you cannot have one without the other. Organisational culture that is built on respect and integrity has far fewer hurdles to overcome when it comes to performance. This is particularly true for organisations such as the RFDS where both these attributes are inextricably linked and it becomes self-evident at the front line of service.

How do you personally balance the power you have as a leader with the respect you show to those you lead?

My style is one of being open, honest and collaborative. I am the CEO, but that doesn't mean I'm the one with all the best ideas.

People want to be heard and to know that their opinion counts. I always encourage my team to ask for clarification or to sug-gest ideas. While I can't always say *yes*, I will always listen and consider ideas on merit. I believe people understand and respect this.

Do you have a strategy for sound decision-making? This might include creating a time and environment that allows you to make good decisions.

The first thing I would say is that you must take the time to gather as much information from a number of sources as you can. When it comes to making important decisions, being able to view the issue from multiple vantage points, using reliable information, will give you the best opportunity for a successful outcome.

When making decisions, I always reflect on great pieces of advice I was given by leaders whom I have learned from:

- Trust your instincts. If it smells wrong, it probably is.
- The worst decision to make is no decision at all. Gather the information available at the time and make your best valued decision; it may not always be right, but it will always be better than doing nothing. People follow leaders who make decisions.
- You can't be right all the time. It's very important that you're prepared to acknowledge a wrong call, face up to it and learn from it.
- Decisions need to be made for the best interest of the whole organisation. This won't always make you popular – and that's OK.

Chapter 6

SELF-AWARENESS

Margot Smith

Everything that irritates us about others can
lead us to an understanding of ourselves.

C.G. Jung

Author note

One of the undoubted highlights of the Institute's first bestselling book – Leadership Matters – 7 skills of very successful leaders, *the prequel to Leading Well – was Margot Smith's chapter 'Networking is Working'. It was certainly one of the chapters that I received most feedback about.*

Margot returns here with an equally absorbing consideration of what I believe is fast-becoming the 'new frontier' in management and leadership development: Self-awareness.

Over the last decade or so, self-awareness has made its way from the lecture halls of university psychology departments to take centre stage in HR departments and play a leading part in their approach to culture transformation.

Leaders today are expected to be aware of their own strengths and weaknesses, but it's more than that. Successful leaders are expected to be open to the personal change process that lies at the heart of self-awareness. Knowing yourself isn't enough – striving to better yourself is increasingly what differentiates great leadership from good leadership.

In this chapter, Margot describes the journey that is self-awareness. She describes this journey as a journey of change for a leader – a journey of change that is at the same time incredibly challenging and immensely rewarding.

SELF-AWARENESS IS the first step towards becoming a successful leader. I know that the authors of other chapters of this book argue that their specific attribute is the hallmark of a successful leader, but I agree with the leading emotional intelligence expert and prominent American psychologist, Daniel Goleman, who says that, *'If your emotional abilities aren't in hand – if you don't have self-awareness – then no matter how smart you are, you are not going to get very far.'*[1]

Successful leaders are self-aware. Having a strong understanding of who you are and what impact you are having on those around you is crucial to being effective in your leadership role, and in your life.

In this chapter, I explore the pivotal role that self-awareness plays in sound leadership. Of course, I will acknowledge that self-awareness alone is not enough to be a successful leader. It is not enough to think or say, *'I know that I'm blunt (or aggressive or overly passive).'* Self-awareness lies at the beginning of the process, but without action – and, of course, change – it is relatively useless.

In that sense, I present self-awareness as part of the leadership journey. My view is that it is *the* crucial part, the route planner, the Google Maps. Self-awareness is the foundation on which good leadership is built. It is the leadership attribute that provides the light for the other six attributes covered in this book to shine.

THE BEATING HEART OF SELF-AWARENESS

Authenticity is a key part of self-awareness. So it makes sense that this chapter follows on from Allison Keogh's authenticity chapter (Chapter 5) and I recommend you read them sequentially.

There is no doubt that people will catch on if you are 'faking it' as a leader. When I first started performance-managing staff, I absolutely dreaded it. To manage my dread, I would prepare copious notes and have these in front of me as an actor has her script when she is rehearsing for a play. During one of these particularly memorable early performance discussions with a team member, I sat there with a long list of typed bullet points, reading monotonously through my very one-sided script. On the odd occasion, I would look up, but I was so focused on 'getting through' the pre-prepared script that I didn't see or hear the responses of the staff member. It was a performance conversation, and my own performance was terrible!

Time and practice (and increased self-awareness!) have taught me that the very best performance-management discussions are those where I am completely in the moment with my staff members. These days, I rarely use notes because I know my staff well and I am fully across their performance. I ensure that I maintain eye contact and connection during the meeting, and I adapt to where the conversation is going.

I had to get through the clunky, rehearsed discussions to grow and learn as a leader. Being an authentic leader and being aware of how you work and how you best communicate is essential.

Another example from my own experiences is how I need to work on my presentation skills and work-related speeches. These had been my Achilles heel for some time. Around two years ago, my leader brought this to my attention after a presentation to the board. At my manager's prompting I attended a presentation skills course and I practised and practised. I also realised that I needed to change the way I approached presenting. I needed to prepare thoroughly, rather than simply thinking that I could stand at the front, read from prepared notes and hope I got through the next 45 minutes without totally freezing up.

While I know I'm never going to be the next Simon Sinek – ad-libbing and delivering lengthy speeches – I do have my own style now and I get much better feedback about that style than I once did. These days I can even adapt my script mid-presentation or ad-lib when needed or when I'm asked a tricky question.

Like the change in my approach to performance-management conversations with staff, this change began with self-awareness. I realised that I was falling short and that I wasn't being my true, authentic self. I realised that I was selling myself short and letting myself (and my team and my audience) down. I needed to make a change – and I resolved to make that change. Self-awareness is often found at the very beginning of the change process. It is where insight intersects with a desire to take action.

If there is an area of your leadership style or an aspect of how you lead that requires work or development it is absolutely crucial to take input from others, to observe what they do well and what they do differently to you; to picture role models who do 'it' well and think about how they perform in given situations. Of course, this isn't about trying to overlay someone else's style on top of yours. It's about asking, observing and learning. It's then about adding your own unique style, your own stories and your own approach.

The process begins with the realisation and acceptance that change is required; that is the beating heart of self-awareness.

THE JOHARI WINDOW MODEL OF SELF-AWARENESS

The Johari Window is a theory of consciousness, but it does offer a practical way to think about your own level of self-awareness. If a particular skill or attribute is known to others and known to you, it's 'open' or public knowledge. For example, this might be your fantastic attention to detail or inability to multi-task. Individuals can build trust between themselves by sharing information with others and learning about others from the details they share about themselves.

Interestingly, the underlying assumption of the Johari Window model is that the effectiveness of our personal communication increases as this window – this openness – becomes larger.[2]

The model shown in Figure 6.1 below illustrates that there may be things that are unknown to you but that are known to others; these are referred to as 'blind spots'. It might be that you are incredibly thoughtful and that this has been observed by others as a particular strength. However, you may not actually realise this about yourself.

Your ability to work on a blind spot is of course inhibited if you are not actually aware that the blind spot exists. How do you know that people regard you as incredibly thoughtful?

Blind spots are typically realised through feedback. It is important to ask for feedback, both formally with surveys or during performance discussions (yours and your team's), as well as informally. For example, you might seek informal feedback in the kitchen at work or after a meeting that went particularly well or particularly badly.

Figure 6.1 – The Johari Window of Self-awareness model

	Known to self	*Unknown to self*
Known to others	**OPEN** Public knowledge *What I show* *to you*	**BLIND** Feedback *Your gift to me*
Unknown to others	**HIDDEN** Private *Mine to share* *if I trust you*	**UNCONSCIOUS** Unknown *New awareness* *can emerge*

Seeking and receiving feedback is at the core of the Johari Window model and is key to why the model is so powerful in terms of increasing self-awareness. It's worth pointing out straight away that seeking, receiving and indeed giving feedback takes courage. It is absolutely critical that you ensure that those you ask for feedback feel as safe as possible sharing their observations. Ultimately, you will benefit from the feedback and the potential exposure of blind spots, so as a leader you must ensure that all feedback is gratefully received.

In soliciting feedback from others, you open yourself up to the possibility that aspects of yourself and your behaviour might move from 'unconscious' or 'unknown' to 'known'. Feedback allows for the possibility that you might overcome some of the areas that may have been inhibiting your leadership style and your leadership development.

The bottom left quadrant of the Johari Window is the 'hidden' area. There are aspects of you and your behaviour that are known to you and yet remain unknown – or hidden – to others. For example, you might have a rather jealous streak and be quite resentful of one of your colleagues who is in the process of getting a promotion, but you are not comfortable sharing these feelings with others.

Lastly, the 'unconscious' parts of you are both unknown to you and also unknown to others. You might, for example, have a morbid fear of snakes which, until you see an actual snake, you are unaware of. Or you might be great at assessing risks in an organisation, but until you have to prepare a risk management plan, you won't be aware of this and it will remain an untapped skill.

The Johari Window in practice

Blind spots can be uncovered. Indeed, self-awareness is the journey that identifies, acknowledges and tackles blind spots.

Early in my management and leadership career, I received feedback from my manager that I really needed to work on my empathy. She told me that she observed that I sometimes struggled to understand what people in my team were going through, and empathy was a crucial leadership attribute.

This feedback was incredibly powerful. It had quite a profound effect on me. Sometimes when you need to develop a skill or an aspect of your leadership style it's because actually you don't value it. If you don't put too much importance on being punctual, for example, you won't make a conscious effort to be on time for meetings or engagements. So, you can imagine the soul searching I went through when I was told that I was effectively not an empathetic leader!

Self-awareness is about this type of soul searching. I first had to acknowledge that this observation from my manager was in fact true. For a period of time, if I'm being completely honest, I did convince myself that she was wrong; I was totally empathetic and she simply didn't know me. I didn't agree with this feedback, because *I saw myself* as an empathetic person. My friends thought I was empathetic, my image and understanding of my character was that I was an empathetic person. But since I was in my late twenties and had all the answers, I wasn't bringing my whole self to work. I thought the 'work me' was meant to be different from the 'home me'. The truth was that I wasn't being what Allison describes in Chapter 5 as an authentic leader.

I was very fortunate that my manager suggested I participate in an emerging leaders' development program. This program was a huge learning curve for me. It proved to make the difference between me forging a leadership path of self-awareness or a path of self-destruction.

Of course, I'm not saying that I'm now a perfectly empathetic leader – far from it. I am saying that the tools and insights I gained in that program were career-changing. They caused me to ask myself some tough questions and to start on the path towards conscious competence as a leader.

What exactly did I learn about empathy on the emerging leaders' development program?

I learnt something extremely valuable. I learnt that my apparent lack of empathy in my early days as a new manager stemmed from my own leadership journey. It's true that I haven't had a smooth or speedy road to success. I worked hard to get my first leadership role. I saw myself as very busy and perfectly able to deal with whatever work threw at me. Unfortunately, this led me at times to feel that others were not able to cope – I questioned why they couldn't push through things in the same way I was able to. When my manager said that I wasn't empathetic, it felt to me as if I was being punished for being productive, effective and resilient. If someone in the team couldn't meet a deadline or was struggling to cope, why should I put up with that? Or worse, why should I be the one to take on the work? After all, I was coping!

Of course, this was all the very definition of lacking empathy! As I said, the emerging leaders' development course was really quite confronting for me.

At the time – and quite rightly – this realisation was both hor- rifying and a bit embarrassing. I had some people around me going through some challenging issues, but I didn't have the maturity, empathy or compassion to stop and truly appreciate that. Irrespective of the impact on me and my workload, their wellbeing or confidence or whatever, was, or at least should have been, paramount.

Fortunately, self-awareness opens up the pathway to change. Following the development program, I set about thinking through the ways that I could tackle this part of my leadership style (of me!) that I hadn't known existed. How could I become more empathetic?

One practical way was to start doing voluntary charity work. I felt that this would give me real insight into what others were going through and the different journeys that people were on in their lives. I also felt that I really needed to tackle this idea that I hadn't 'had it easy'. Perhaps the truth was that I had.

I started to volunteer, and this really opened my eyes and my mind to the life situations of others. I volunteered with a charity taking clients with a disability on outings (picture yourself commentating on intimate movie scenes to a vision impaired person!). I was also involved for about six years with a charity that offers respite to HIV+ kids through activity camps. The camps were held twice a year and they were always a highlight for me. They allowed me to give back – but also offered me incredible insight into how blessed my journey has been and my own life actually is.

In parallel to this I actively made a few very simple changes. I made a conscious effort to engage in active listening at work. Rather than judging and comparing situations to my own life experience, I started to see that people's stories were their own.

These days I am a much better leader because of these things. While I shudder to think of how hard and cold I was in the early days, I must take heart in the fact that I was also a product of my circumstances – and I was willing to change. I was willing to accept that what I was doing just wasn't serving me well anymore; and it certainly wasn't serving those around me. I'm thankful that I learnt this lesson at twenty-something, but I firmly believe that improving self-awareness is a process that is just as applicable at sixty-something.

THE IMPORTANCE OF PROFESSIONAL DEVELOPMENT

My own journey of self-awareness is personal and might bear little resemblance to yours, but one thing is constant: managers and leaders need to seek out leadership development opportunities. These include mentoring, coaching, reading management and leadership books, blogs and publications, formal study and qualifications, and of course joining industry bodies such as the Institute of Managers and Leaders (IML).

Insight about yourself and about your impact on others can come from many different sources, but if you aren't 'plugged in' to these sources you're left with few external feeds to rely on. As in my own example, I thought that I was the most empathetic leader around. It was only when I was told otherwise that I began to question my leadership style.

That's the thing about leadership: you are never 'done'. It is your responsibility to seek out ways and means to develop yourself. Self-awareness isn't an end point or a destination, it's a pathway. It's the key to unlocking your true potential.

ANALYTICS AND SELF-AWARENESS

Self-awareness and reflection go hand-in-hand. In recent years, the access to tools that can facilitate reflection has grown significantly. Where once there was Myers–Briggs and very little else, today Myers–Briggs and a plethora of other analytical tools are widely available. These analytical tools can be incredibly valuable in enabling you to both self-assess and gather feedback from peers, managers, your team, family and business and non-business networks. If you are keen to understand yourself and to use the views of others as a platform on which to build self-awareness, then there are plenty of tools available to help you do this.

However, one option stands out from the crowd. In my view and from my own experience as a leader (and in the view of the IML), it's the option that lies at the very heart of self-awareness analysis – the 360-degree feedback tool.

It was David Pich, the CEO of the Institute, who said at a national conference of HR leaders, *'If you're not doing 360-degree feedback yourself and with your team it's close to impossible to claim that you're a self-aware leader'.*

The 360-degree feedback process helps you and your team to identify strengths, discover weaknesses, face challenges and uncover areas that you need to develop. It is, by equal measure, challenging and rewarding. It certainly isn't easy. In fact, in my experience, I would say that it requires something akin to a leap of faith, but it is absolutely fundamental to understanding yourself and to understanding how you are perceived by others. Only when these two perspectives are known can change and personal growth follow.

The IML 360 Analytical Tool – a catalyst for change

The IML 360 tool is one of the most popular self-awareness focused analytical products available to organisations to assist in creating better managers and leaders for a better society.

IML 360 is based on the IML Competency Framework and ultimately by the same framework that supports the globally prestigious Chartered Manager designation (CMgr). It measures leaders on how they:

- Manage and lead self;
- Manage and lead others; and
- Manage and lead the business.

It surveys respondents who are asked to rate the participant on the frequency of demonstrated behaviours that are fully aligned to the competency framework.

The Institute's research that underpins the design of the IML 360 tool offers fascinating insight into the top five strengths and the top five weaknesses of leaders, as well as the most common blind spots.

Top five strengths of leaders

According to leaders/participants	Area	Score (out of 5)
Provide governance	Manage business	4.9
Manage and value diversity	Manage others	4.8
Promote equality of opportunity, diversity and inclusion	Manage business	4.6
Manage financial resources	Manage business	4.5
Manage human resources	Manage business	4.5

According to observers	Area	Score (out of 5)
Provide governance	Manage business	4.7
Manage and value diversity	Manage others	4.6
Promote equality of opportunity, diversity and inclusion	Manage business	4.5
Manage financial resources	Manage business	4.4
Recruit, select, induct and retain people	Manage others	4.4

Top five areas of weakness/need for development

According to leaders/participants	Area	Score (out of 5)
Develop creative and innovative thinking	Manage self	3.7
Develop individuals	Manage others	3.9
Manage conflict	Manage others	4.0
Influence and negotiation skills	Manage others	4.0
Develop decision-making and problem-solving skills	Manage self	4.1

According to observers	Area	Score (out of 5)
Develop creative and innovative thinking	Manage self	3.9
Develop individuals	Manage others	3.9
Manage conflict	Manage others	4.0
Develop decision-making and problem-solving skills	Manage self	4.1
Influence and negotiation skills	Manage others	4.1

Blind spots (gap in leader vs observer scores)

Top five strengths	Area	Gap
Develop creative and innovative thinking	Manage self	0.1
Recruit, select, induct and retain people	Manage others	0.1
Influence and negotiation skills	Manage others	0.1
Cultivate business acumen – seeing the bigger picture	Manage self	0.1
Delegate effectively	Manage others	0.0

Top five areas of weakness/need for development	Area	Gap
Develop and implement your organisation's vision, values and culture	Manage business	-0.3
Provide governance	Manage business	-0.2
Manage and value diversity	Manage others	-0.2
Manage human resources	Manage business	-0.2
Manage financial resources	Manage business	-0.2

It's interesting to note that governance and diversity score highly among both leaders themselves and observers. This could be because these areas are more black and white. Compliance with the HR processes when hiring or applying fairness across the diverse members of the team are typically 'yes' or 'no' responses, and thankfully seem to be strong.

However, when it comes to creativity, conflict and influencing skills, the picture is not so rosy. These traits are harder and undoubtedly more difficult to attain. The results indicate that leaders have considerable work to do in the following areas:

- Developing creative and innovative thinking
- Developing individuals
- Managing conflict
- Developing decision-making and problem-solving skills
- Influence and negotiation skills.

The IML 360 tool also focuses on leadership blind spots. It is intriguing to note that, given governance, HR, finance and diversity all appear as the top five strengths, they are also viewed as blind spots. It is certainly the case that a leader can be strong in a specific area and yet there can still be a gap between how good they think they are in this area and how strong they are perceived to be by others.

Tools like the IML 360 are designed to help you to recognise your blind spots, but also to reinforce your strengths or development areas. They are an invaluable resource for managers and leaders seeking to become more self-aware and ultimately to be better managers and leaders.

SELF-AWARENESS AND GENDER

It's time now for me to tackle an important topic that has become more important since in recent months the #metoo movement has reverberated around the world and throughout the workplace.

As a woman in the workplace I learnt an important lesson in self-awareness a number of years ago. When I moved into my early management and leadership roles, I increasingly found that I needed to check myself when I was asked to do certain things by the people I worked for – or even by my colleagues. On more than one occasion (many more than one!) I was asked to get the coffee or to write the minutes in meetings. Unfortunately, in the first few years, I did these things without questioning why it always seemed to be me who was being asked. I saw it as being helpful or even worse, a sign that I was needed.

Over time, as I became more confident and more aware of my position (and the fact that it was always me who was being asked!), I began to feel that it shouldn't always be me. Of course, that's not to say I *never* get the water and glasses for a meeting or offer to grab the coffees or take the minutes. I do. In fact, I ensure that I often offer to do these things. But I frequently and actively stop and think – are they asking because I am a woman, because they never ask the man sitting next to me, or are they asking because I am a person and an equal to all the others in the room?

I'm not saying, don't take the minutes or offer to get the coffees. But think, why are *you* doing it? Or why is someone asking *you* to do it?

In the same way, this form of self-awareness applies to all forms of diversity and inclusion. It's critical to understand that self-awareness is about recognising that you don't always know what it's like to walk in someone else's shoes. As such, it's important to ensure that you don't speak on behalf of others ('mansplaining' is an absolute no-no, of course) and don't read too much into body language because this is a notoriously poor indicator of anything.

Self-awareness is about asking questions, listening to the answers and offering people a platform to speak, contribute and be heard.

SELF-AWARENESS – BEING YOUR VERY BEST SELF

Gaining and improving self-awareness is tough. Behavioural change is hard work, and behavioural change that is focused on areas that perhaps you didn't know needed to change is even tougher. That's what self-awareness is all about. If it's any consolation, the alternative is actually even tougher. Leading in a bubble or a vacuum and leaving leadership destruction in your wake is no fun at all. It's worth remembering that people typically leave bosses not workplaces.

The 2018 IML National Salary Survey found that 25.8% of surveyed organisations stated 'conflict with staff/manager' was a main reason for staff leaving the organisation. Gallup has an even more staggering statistic – it purports that around half of the employees they surveyed left a job to 'get away from their manager'.[3]

We all have a responsibility to be the best boss and work colleague we can be.

In fact, when it comes to self-awareness, there's actually more to it than that. Surely, we all want to be our very best self? And, surely, we want to look back on our work and on our workplaces and think we had an impact and made a contribution – however large or small – and that we developed ourselves and others along the way.

To be clear, this doesn't mean that we need to go 'all Zen' and start hanging crystals around the office! It also doesn't mean that we won't be impacted by the feedback we seek and receive; we will. Feedback does have an impact. It's supposed to have. Our role as self-aware leaders is to do our very best to receive it with grace and to accept it and act on it.

How do you move towards being your best self?

Here are my top five tips:

1. Use the tools at your disposal to understand what a successful leader looks and acts like – and work towards it. See the self-awareness checklist or action plan later in the chapter for some tips to move into action mode.

2. Keep in mind you won't develop all the time. There will be ebbs and flows; times when you are working hard on developing. Perhaps you are developing financial acumen and being mentored by your finance manager, doing a course, or reading up on financial management, and the result is you've increased your knowledge and skills.

3. It's OK to have a break from professional growth to dedicate time to friends or family because you and they need some quality time. Then you might tackle procrastination. Actually, it's best to put that one off... (sorry, that's a very old and well used self-awareness joke).

4. Consider the circumstances in which you are your best self. Are there certain circumstances that stop you in your tracks and put you in a positive frame of mind?

5. Write down the changes you want to make. I know this sounds a bit like pop psychology, but the truth is that writing things down and reviewing them regularly has a funny way of holding us to account.

There's lazy and then there's lazy! The paradox of the lazy leader

Ian Mathieson FIML argues that there's a strong case for the right type of laziness in leading

The notion that laziness among leaders is not necessarily a bad thing was first attributed to General Helmuth von Moltke, Chief of the German General Staff between 1857 and 1887. The General had observed that, in some cases, the leaders who were most often described as being lazy were typically those who applied themselves and ultimately delivered the very best value to the organisation. In other words, perhaps what was observed as laziness was actually not laziness at all, but the ultimate in business efficiency. This observation and the theory that grew from it was originally applied to the military, but arguably it can be applied equally to the workplace.

At its simplest, the notion of the lazy leader is about self-awareness and efficiency at work. General von Moltke had noticed that the leaders who were often labelled as lazy had attracted this label because they tended to focus their attention and action on a small number of things and, in parallel, they tended to delegate most of the other tasks outside of the few they focused on. Interestingly, the tasks they chose to focus on were those that they were well aware they were good at, whereas they delegated those tasks they recognised they didn't excel at themselves, or which others could deliver more effectively.

As such, from a leadership perspective, the lazy leaders were actually the leaders who were focused on doing those things only they could do, and could do well. They recruited and attracted the right staff who would focus on the other things that needed doing, and doing well. As such, the organisation as a whole tended to perform better. The paradox was that so-called lazy leaders created organisations where the best and brightest wanted to work.

While this was observed by others as being a sign of laziness, it was actually the ultimate in self-awareness and efficiency. From the leader's perspective, they knew themselves well enough to realise what they could deliver well and when they needed help. The lazy leaders tended to have absolutely no issues in saying that they couldn't do something or saying that they needed help. In fact, they frequently asked for help! This may have been viewed by others as a sign of weakness (or laziness), but the performance of the team tended to improve with each call for help.

Characteristics of a lazy leader

They treat strategy as live and dynamic.

- Strategy is not an annual process.
- It requires constant awareness, readiness and flexibility to review strategies when the environment changes in ways that impact the organisation.
- Significant change doesn't restrict itself to an annual cycle, neither should strategy.
- A lazy leader will nurture this awareness among their senior team and throughout the organisation.

They only do the things they are really good at, or have to do.

- This requires clarity about which roles the person will exercise and those they won't.
- It requires considerable reflection, discipline, personal insight and personal mastery.
- It requires careful selection, especially of the direct reports.
- The lazy leader needs to select the right direct reports, trust them and keep in touch with them about what they are doing.
- There's a lot of trust in this – informed trust, not blind trust.

They coach their people.

- Lazy leaders encourage a coaching culture throughout the organisation.
- They see coaching is an investment, not a sunk cost.

In an interview, Jack Welch, former CEO of GE, said that one of his important roles was coaching his direct reports (who were very senior and highly-paid executives). He said that he encouraged a two-way coaching relationship with his team, that he had things to learn from them.

They admit their mistakes.

- There's nowhere to hide when there's a stuff-up.
- Eventually if not quickly, stuff-ups by a leader join the Worst-Kept-Secret Club.
- Denying a stuff-up most likely perpetuates the problem and increases the damage.
- Early acknowledgement helps the team to focus on solutions and remedies.

They assess performance holistically and not just on numbers.

- Numbers are important, but they often camouflage efforts, inputs and achievements that warrant identification and analysis.
- Achieving an easy target is different to achieving a target that confronted serious challenges. This warrants more than a tick.
- Evaluating key relationships – customers, suppliers, regulators, others of significance – is important. Assessing performance in these contexts sometimes is numeric, sometimes it's not.
- It requires courage and clarity to go beyond numbers.

They observe and actively participate as little as possible.

- Staying out of the game most of the time opens up opportunities for fresh insight from others.
- Open dialogue provides opportunities among the staff for growth.
- They are only decisive when it is essential. Mostly the direct reports and their reports have excellent information and will make good decisions.

They embrace complexity and debate real alternatives.

- Being decisive is the last resort. Lazy leaders encourage debate; often the decision that emerges is the one the lazy leader would have made but the process creates more buy-in than a handed-down decision.
- As with strategy, constant awareness, readiness and flexibility encourage the best in others.
- Synthesis is the fifth discipline espoused by Peter Senge.[4] It encompasses both left-brain and right-brain capacities.

They take a long-term view and reflect both personally and collectively with the team.

- Time to reflect is essential to a lazy leader; they ensure there's time for them to review and reflect. It's a key element in personal mastery.
- Reflecting includes opening up to enable left-field or subconscious thoughts to come into play.
- Reflection readily occurs in conversations, especially when the right conversation is led that way.
- The lazy leader ensures there's time to reflect with their direct reports and with other significant groups.
- Engaging with customers about where they are going and how they see the future can provide valuable reflection space.
- Reflective engagement with the team enhances team performance and collective team-learning.

They ensure that there is a line of sight to the customer throughout the organisation.

- The organisation benefits when everyone in it knows that customers are the core of the organisation's being. No matter how far from the coalface a staff member is, goods are produced and services provided for customers.
- Everyone, not just the sales and accounts departments, should have a line of sight to the customer.

- The lazy leader doesn't tolerate leaders and senior teams who are 'too busy' for customers or 'too focused on my stuff; leave that to marketing' to keep line of sight with customers.

They listen thoroughly and carefully across a wide spectrum of views and opinions.

- Lazy leaders are good and patient, attentive listeners.
- They hesitate to put views and offer opinions; they hesitate to be decisive.

I'm conscious that this might appear to be a heck of a list, but if we take the ten key elements of lazy leadership we end up with the following:

1. They treat strategy as live and dynamic.
2. They only do the things they are really good at, or have to do.
3. They coach their people.
4. They admit their mistakes.
5. They assess performance holistically and not just on numbers.
6. They observe and actively participate as little as possible.
7. They embrace complexity and debate real alternatives.
8. They take a long-term view and they reflect both personally and collectively with the team.
9. They ensure that there is a line of sight to the customer throughout the organisation.
10. They listen thoroughly and carefully across a wide spectrum of views and opinions.

It seems to me from this list that lazy leadership, far from being a negative archetype, is actually a formula for sound leadership.

So, treat this as a 'smorgasbord' – self-evaluate the points on the list and reflect. Complement insights with realistic evaluation of your strengths and weaknesses. Do any areas or focuses spring to mind for you to start your journey?

Identify the goals you plan to achieve in those areas, then set targets for skills development. Plan support measures. Is there any helpful literature? Can you get some coaching or mentoring? Are there any relevant courses you could consider doing?

It's a journey more than a destination. Persistence and dedication, supported by personal reflection, facilitate the journey.

LIGHTS, CAMERA, ACTION!

Now that you've decided to make a change, what can you expect to happen next? How do you translate awareness and intention into that all-important action that you and your team want to see so that you can be a better leader? These questions are especially pertinent if the behaviour you are working on has been a blind spot for you in the past.

Stephen Covey is famously quoted as saying, *'We judge ourselves by our intentions and others by their behaviour.'*[5] This is an important sentiment to grasp because in order to show a noticeable change, you may need to really step up how you demonstrate the change you are trying to make. After all, the proof of the pudding is in the eating, and self-awareness is only powerful when it is illustrated by demonstrable change.

The first step in demonstrating change is often to share with your team that you are working on a particular area. If, for example, you have discovered a blind spot around active listening (from doing the IML 360!), you could start by telling your team that you have had some feedback that you need to develop in this area and you would like their help to identify when you could be doing this better.

This achieves two purposes: your team immediately sees that you are prepared to be honest and vulnerable with them, and they see that you are actually interested in developing yourself – both great leadership qualities in themselves.

Once you have disclosed the area that you are committed to working on, you can then go a step further and ask for ways in which your team – or the people who gave you the feedback – can help you develop in that area. In the example of active listening, they might suggest that they will offer feedback to you when you are slipping into bad habits and not demonstrating active listening. Or they might offer to introduce you to someone they know who is really good at listening who can give you some tips over coffee. Or perhaps they might suggest a book that really helped them in this area.

Whatever the suggestion, by opening yourself up to the possibility of change and by allowing your team to play a part in the process, real action can take place.

Let's be clear here: when I say *'lights, camera, action'*, I really do mean it. You need to be prepared for the fact that you will be in the spotlight. Once you have started the process of self-awareness, all eyes will be on you and on your behaviour. So, when you say you are going to work on your active listening skills, you need to remember that your team will be observing your behaviour not your intentions. The best intentions in the world are easily destroyed by actions that contradict them.

One tip here is to explain to your team that the change you are undertaking is likely to take some time and that there may be a few failures along the way. After all, the behaviour you are working on has likely been in place for many years.

Here is a checklist to consider some ways in which you might approach taking action to make a change.

A simple self-awareness checklist or action plan

- ☐ Is your manager or a colleague in your corner?
- ☐ Do you have a mentor or coach?
- ☐ Seek feedback – qualitative or quantitative, or both (via a survey or conversations).
- ☐ Engage with the feedback, acknowledge its truth.
- ☐ Identify two or three areas to develop and move into action mode.
- ☐ Ask for help (examples of where you have displayed x and how to get to y). Ask friends and colleagues/your boss to keep you honest and offer ideas and support.
- ☐ Read articles on development areas. Follow relevant LinkedIn or Facebook groups for tips, attend events on the subject, enrol in a webinar, etc.
- ☐ Seek out role models who are good at your gaps – think about what they would do.
- ☐ Check in on your progress after a while and seek more feedback on whether your trusted adviser has seen a change and adjust accordingly.
- ☐ Practise, practise, practise.

THE FINAL WORD ON SELF-AWARENESS

There is absolutely no doubt that increasing your self-awareness takes considerable courage. You are going to need to be prepared to ask yourself and those around you some very tough questions – and that's only the beginning. Once you have discovered the answers you are going to need to be prepared to do some hard work.

Self-awareness is so critical precisely because it is so hard. The fact is that many leaders aren't focused on self-awareness, which is why the payback for a truly self-aware leader can be so high. You measure the payback not only in staff retention and engagement, but in the level of your own self-esteem and in the relationships you form with your team.

There is another way of looking at the subject of self-awareness, and it's this: why would you want to continue to do the same thing as a leader if some aspects of what you are doing are not doing you any favours? Surely, it's best to find out what these aspects are and change them – for your own development and for the benefit of your team.

Back when I was discovering that I had a blind spot around my ability to show empathy, my manager said to me that if I kept doing what I had been doing, I'd keep getting the results I'd been getting! It sounds so obvious now, but so many leaders will ignore the signs and markers or refuse to ask the questions that will ultimately lead to them becoming better leaders. They keep doing what they have always done. To focus on improving your self-awareness is to reject this cycle and to commit to self-improvement.

Self-awareness is the ultimate personal continual improvement process for a leader.

My advice is that leaders make the commitment to becoming more self-aware – now.

Chapter 7

DECISIVENESS

Bill Kernoczy and Luke Challenor

In any moment of decision, the best thing you can do
is the right thing, the next best thing is the wrong thing
and the worst thing you can do is nothing.

Theodore Roosevelt

Author note

It seems glaringly obvious to say that leaders are expected to be decisive and that making decisions is part and parcel of leadership. While leaders have always been, by definition, decision-makers, there is something a little different about modern-day leadership that has seen decisiveness take centre stage as a key leadership attribute. It is the sheer amount of data that today's leaders are faced with and the speed that this data is available. These factors make leadership decision-making so much more critical to businesses, to teams and to individual managers and leaders.

It is for this reason that decisiveness pipped a number of other leadership attributes and sneaked into this book.

Asking Bill Kernoczy and Luke Challenor to contribute this chapter was one of the easier decisions that I had to make. Bill and Luke are both long-standing Members and contributors to the Institute with a background in developing the skills of management professionals and organisational leaders. More recently, Luke has made a significant contribution to the development of IML's newly launched Foundations of Intentional Leadership Development Program that is aimed squarely at emerging leaders and those who have recently taken on a new leadership position. A large part of the success of this program since launch has been the fact that it encourages participants to actively choose to take ownership of their leadership journey. At the Institute we call this 'leading with intent'. It's about learning to weigh up options and deciding which option is the right one for you as a leader and for your team and your business.

This chapter expands on this theme. Bill and Luke demonstrate that making sound decisions in leadership is both critical and achievable through practice and following sound process.

L**EADERSHIP CAN BE** defined in myriad different ways. If that weren't the case, bookshops, bookshelves and social media feeds would be relatively empty! However, regardless of which definition of leadership you subscribe to, bookmark and post to Instagram, there can be little doubt that leaders are expected to make decisions. In fact, it can be argued – and this argument lies at the heart of this chapter – that decisiveness is what sets successful leaders apart. Decisiveness is at the heart of good leadership.

While the art of decision-making and the ability to make the right decision has always been a core element in the day-to-day role of a manager, in the modern workplace, today's leaders are expected to navigate a path through seemingly endless data flows with constant communication, on-demand customer needs and increasing reporting requirements. Decision-making has never been so complex, so time-consuming and so critical. The ability to make good decisions has always been an important aspect of leadership, but it has never been as central, as mission-critical, as career-defining as it is today. Good leaders make good decisions, and they do this almost by default.

This chapter provides a range of practical tools, examples and models to help you progress on your leadership journey by boosting your confidence in making the right decision at the right time.

WHY DO LEADERS NEED TO MAKE DECISIONS?

Well, for starters, it's in every leader's position description to be able to make good decisions! As a manager and a leader your role requires a level of authority and there's an expectation that you will make decisions to keep your team, your department, your business or your multinational company operating productively. Often your manager has delegated that authority to you to ensure their time is better spent on other priorities.

Aside from decision-making being a significant aspect of a leader's job description, there are two primary drivers that compel leaders to make decisions:

- **You need to get things done.** Within your role in the chain of command you will be presented with a process or a problem which needs a decision to enable it to continue on to completion. If you don't make a decision a project may be delayed, supplies might not arrive on time or customer orders may not be fulfilled. Decision-making is key to business production flow.

- **Your team needs leadership.** As a leader, all eyes are on you and regardless of whether you get it right or wrong your team will judge you on your ability to make a decision. As team members we all want to know that our leader is capable of making a decision. We are inspired when our leader shows courage and confidence in making a decision.

HOW DO LEADERS MAKE A DECISION?

As a manager you need some internal process in your brain to help you identify what type of decision needs to be made. This process may rely on previous experience that makes you confidence of a particular result or you might need some additional rational thought to help you make the right choice.

The first decision you need to make is whether you *can* actually make a decision. Once you are presented with a problem or a task you need to quickly determine if you are in the right position to make a decision.

In the first instance, you need to decide if you have the right information available to you. If you do, then you can move on and use your own criteria to follow your decision-making process. If you don't have the right information then your next move is to gain the information necessary for you to then decide if you can make a decision. Figure 7.1 is a visual reminder of this.

Figure 7.1 – Quick check decision-making

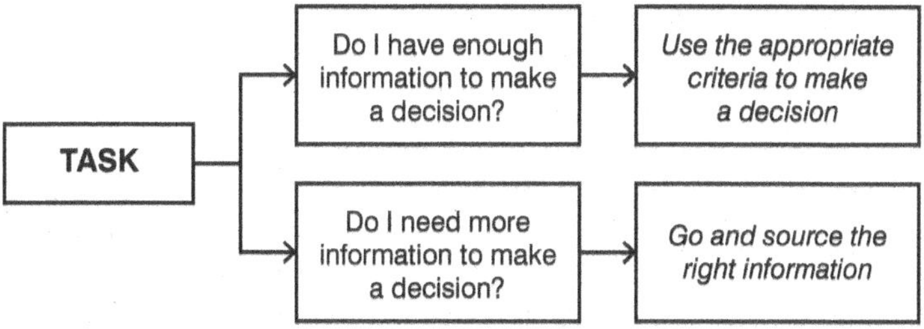

Leaders, stop avoiding hard decisions

Ron Carucci

In his article published in the *Harvard Business Review*[1] Ron Carucci identifies three reasons why leaders avoid making a decision and explains the negatives associated with the inability to make a decision. As a leader you need to understand the consequences of not making a decision and take actions to avoid these excuses.

'I'm being considerate of others.' For some leaders, the thought of estranging those they lead with a difficult call is paralysing. I've heard leaders say things like, 'Morale is already low. I hate to add to their stress.' The real issue is that many leaders don't want to disappoint their people.

'I'm committed to quality and accuracy.' For leaders who struggle with the ambiguity that often comes with decisions that have long-term implications, the anxiety over being wrong can be consuming. They try to impose certainty by analysing more data and soliciting more opinions, but the real issue is their fear of looking stupid.

Taking action in the face of incomplete data is a leader's job. You sometimes won't know if the decision was 'right' until long after it's made. As a leader, you should model taking calculated risks and learning from mistakes.

'I want to be seen as fair.' In a world of headlines about leaders mistreating people with harsh and unfair expectations, and bonuses calculated on employee engagement scores, many leaders fear being seen as uncaring or playing favourites. This has become especially true in a world where everyone gets a 'participation trophy' because leaders falsely believe acknowledging differences in performance is the same as showing different levels of respect. Failing to address underperformance or to acknowledge the great work of your high performers couldn't be more unfair or disrespectful. Differentiating levels of performance is a leader's job. When you avoid decisions that do so, you dilute meritocracy and redefine contribution as merely one's efforts, regardless of outcome. It's unfair to the highest performers whose work likely accounts for a larger percentage of the team's success, and it's cruel to the lowest performers to allow them to flounder in roles for which they are ill prepared.

As a leader, how you make hard calls shapes your organisation's decision-making culture over time. These excuses teach people that self-protection and self-interest are legitimate motivations for making difficult choices. Whatever temporary pain you might incur from making a tough call should pale in comparison to the precedent you set that it's important to put the organisation's success first.

DECISION-MAKING THEORIES

Theories of decision-making abound. While it isn't the intent of this chapter to provide a comprehensive analysis of the numerous theories of how and why people make decisions, it is worth considering the three leading theories. Not least because it is often the case that as leaders we tend to make decisions instinctively and without an understanding of the theoretical basis for the process that we tend to follow.

Crisis management competencies theory outlines three primary leadership aspects, which are reflected in clusters of competencies that are necessary for effective leadership in crisis situations; when decision-making and decisiveness is paramount.

The construct asserts that leaders must be able to engage in pragmatic decision-making under severe time and resource constraints. As major decisions must be made without the opportunity for system reform or long-term improvements, a multitude of factors need to be considered and acted upon quickly, requiring the leader to have exceptional analytic abilities. Further, as soon as the critical decisions can be made, they must be implemented decisively. As the situation evolves, leaders must be flexible and willing to adapt their own directives as required. Because of the magnitude of work to do and decisions to make, leaders in an emergency situation must delegate as extensively as possible.[2]

Protection motivation theory distinguishes between adaptive coping strategies, such as rational problem-solving (seeking out more information, analysing the problem and making an effective plan) and a host of maladaptive strategies such as avoidance (attempts to evade or deny the threat), wishful thinking, fatalism and hopelessness. It approaches the aspect somewhat differently, being organised along two cognitive mediating processes: the threat-appraisal process (maladaptive response rewards versus the perception of threat in terms of severity and vulnerability) and the coping-appraisal process, which evaluates the ability to cope with and avert the threatened danger (through efficacy and response costs). It assumes that these factors combine to form an intervening variable, protection motivation. The output of these appraisal-mediating processes ultimately is the decision.[3]

Conflict theory is a social psychological theory of decision-making. It focuses on the presence or absence of three antecedent conditions to determine reliance on a particular coping pattern when faced with making a decision particularly under stress. These three conditions are:

1. Awareness about serious risks regarding preferred alternatives;
2. Hope of finding a better alternative; and
3. Belief that there is adequate time to search and deliberate before a decision is required.

Where these three conditions are met a vigilant decision-making pattern (allowing rational and sound decision-making) is expected; while defensive avoidance (escaping conflict by procrastinating or shifting responsibility to someone else or constructing wishful rationalisations) or hypervigilance (impulsively seizing upon hastily contrived solutions) is expected to be triggered when there's a belief that there is little prospect of finding a good solution to the dilemma. Individual differences and personality variables have a major influence on predisposition to use one or other of the patterns.[4]

Utilising this model, conflict theory based decision-making skill training was determined effective in increasing self-esteem and a positive coping style in decision-making.[5] Workshops, based on the theory, were found to promote increased confidence in decision-making and less reported use of maladaptive patterns of decision-making.[6]

Notwithstanding your theoretical starting point, as a leader you will be expected to make decisions and you will be judged on and measured against your ability to weigh things up and choose a decision-making process.

Regardless of the arena, whether it is business, politics, military or other, decisiveness is a key factor. The best leaders make sound, defensible decisions in a timely fashion, especially in times of crisis and uncertainty. Leaders that are perceived as indecisive or poor decision-makers will quickly lose the confidence and commitment of their team. Perception of decisiveness has been found to have a pervasive effect on the role satisfaction of team members.[7]

Recent research has discovered that one of the four aspects that defines a successful CEO is the ability to make decisions with speed and conviction, undermining the perception that the best leaders are those who make the best decisions.[8]

According to Richard Branson, decisiveness is key. He highlights that during growth, crisis or dispute there will be an increase in decision-making required and the speed in which these decisions need to be made will also increase. It is crucial for a successful leader to demonstrate confidence and project a calmness surrounding any decision so that those around them can feel in control of a situation.

Winston Churchill has been discussed in depth when it comes to leadership, and his attitude towards decision-making is no exception. Churchill was renowned for his enjoyment of making decisions. He understood that most individuals and organisations were resistant to change and that as a result for many it was an easier option to remain stagnant than to make and act on decisions. Churchill had little fear of making a decision and was always accepting of the consequences of those decisions.[9] He espoused three hallmarks for decision-making:

1. Always keep the central aspect of the problem in sight;
2. Understand how to balance both sides of a decision; and
3. Have the ability to change course if new facts present themselves.

Latest thinking views decision-making not only as one of the main characteristics of effective leadership, but also as a process rather than an isolated event. While the dangers of taking too long to come to a decision are apparent, leaders must also consider the dangers of deciding too quickly.

Similarly, true leaders have the courage to make decisions without unnecessary hesitation, but they are not rash. Decisiveness is the ability to make appropriate decisions in a timely manner. When the need arises, decisive leaders will make decisions using whatever data they have, even if that requires a leap of faith. Decisiveness is a trait that draws heavily upon past experiences to influence how it is implemented.

HOW A DECISION-MAKING MODEL CAN ASSIST YOUR LEADERSHIP STYLE

The reason why leaders often seek to use a model to help their decision-making is because models can provide a level of structure to an otherwise complex and disorganised situation.

The following models should be used as a framework to help provide you with some structure to give you confidence that you have done sufficient thinking to make a good decision.

The seven-step decision-making process

To help your brain make a rational decision you will find it useful to follow some sort of process, such as the seven-step decision-making process. Following this process will help you to feel confident that you have considered and can later justify your decision if needed. The seven steps are shown in Figure 7.2 below.

Figure 7.2 – The seven-step decision-making process

PROCESS	EXAMPLE
Identify the problem clearly	Selecting employee of the month award
Establish the ideal result	Team member feels recognised and motivated
Determine your criteria	Completing tasks and helping others
Create some options	Potentially Tom, Sue and Jill qualify
Evaluate your options against your criteria	Sue has met all criteria
Implement the most appropriate option	Provide award to Sue
Evaluate results	Sue is feeling rewarded and motivated

Here's how it works. You need to map out each element of the process.

Step 1: Identify the problem clearly

In this step you are trying to define what the problem is that you are attempting to solve. You need to determine what has caused the problem and you also want to confirm that you are the right person to be solving it or making the decision. Do you have the appropriate authority to be making this decision?

Step 2: Establish the ideal result

Next, work out what the ideal result will look like. This is important because you need to know the best outcome and if that is not possible you have to decide what outcomes are likely. Once you know the best outcome possible you can use this as a framework for building the best solution.

Step 3: Determine your criteria

For this process to work effectively you need to be confident that you are using the most appropriate decision-making criteria. This could be factors such as:

- Time – when does it need to be done by?
- Cost – do we have budget allocated?
- Quality – are there agreed quality standards to achieve?
- Customer – are there specific service levels which need to be met?
- Risks – what is the impact of this decision?

Step 4: Create some options

In this step you need to generate some options that will potentially be suitable. It is always good to give yourself two or three alternatives to choose from. You can involve your team in this process to help generate the best possible solution. If the situation has happened previously you can refer back to those options and work out what worked and what didn't work in the past.

Step 5: Evaluate your options against your criteria

Use your criteria to evaluate each of the options in terms of how well they will achieve the end result. You will need to include a mini risk analysis to predict how likely each option is to succeed and what would happen if it doesn't work.

If the decision-making process is complex and uses more than three criteria it might be worth building a matrix and mapping out each option so you can assess them all together.

Once you have assessed your options you are then in a position to select the most appropriate solution.

Alternatively, at this point you might find you require more information or would like to refer the decision to someone who has more experience than you. If this is the case then you need to brief the other person with as much information as you can and explain what criteria and what options you have considered so far.

Step 6: Implement the most appropriate option

Once you have made a decision you need to communicate it to the required stakeholders and then implement it. Make sure all relevant stakeholders know what you decided and be prepared to explain your reasons if required. Check to see that your decision has been implemented correctly.

Step 7: Evaluate results

Decision-making is an important learning process so it becomes especially important to evaluate your decisions and see what worked and what didn't work. Firstly, if the decision worked well, then you should reflect on the criteria and process you followed so that you can make the same decision more efficiently next time. More importantly, if the decision turns out to be incorrect then you need to learn why. Find out why it wasn't correct and identify what criteria or what options you should consider next time. You can involve your staff in the evaluation also, this can be a good group learning opportunity.

The pros and cons analysis

A pros and cons analysis is a simple tool to help you weigh up the positives and negatives of a particular course of action. While you can follow this model on your own it is more effective to involve other stakeholders, especially if they are going to be impacted by the decision.

To use this decision-making model you need to draw up a T-chart with two sides. At the very top write the option you are considering. Under one side list all the benefits of that particular option. On the other side, list all the negatives associated with choosing that option.

When you have generated the lists for the pros and cons go and look through each list and decide how important each point is. This is called weighting.

Once you have weighed up each side you are in a position to determine if the pros outweigh the cons, and if so then can you proceed with that option. If the cons are more significant than the pros you need to look through the cons and see if any of them can be reduced or mitigated. If not, you don't proceed with that option.

Figure 7.3 shows a manager's decision whether to invest in redesigning and purchasing new uniforms for their organisation. The manager might decide that the pros outweigh the cons and so they will proceed with the project.

Figure 7.3 – Example pros and cons decision-making process

Decision: Should we redesign and purchase new staff uniforms?

PROS	CONS
• Staff look more smart and stylish • Customers experience new fresh look • Aligns with new brand image • Modernises the look of employees • More comfortable designs	• Expensive • Time consuming • Some staff might prefer old uniform

SWOT analysis

Leaders will often use a SWOT analysis (Strengths, Weaknesses, Opportunities and Threats) as part of their strategic planning but the same model can also be used to help choose a particular project or task to implement.

SWOT analysis is designed in a way to allow you to think more broadly about implementing a decision. It enables you to determine if an option is viable based on the strengths and weaknesses of an organisation. It also identifies the potential beneficial opportunities and the threats which you might have to face.

A SWOT analysis is a brainstorming framework often laid out as a matrix (see Figure 7.4).

Figure 7.4 – Example SWOT analysis

STRENGTHS	WEAKNESSES
• Good skillset among team members • Excellent training resources available • Good access to decision-makers • High staff engagement	• Outdated equipment • Poor communication across divisions • Staff suffering from change fatigue • Budgets being reduced
OPPORTUNITIES	THREATS
• Saving money and resources which could be allocated to other areas of the business • Improving customer experience • Improving employee experience • Increasing your competitive value proposition • Being seen as a market leader	• Exceeding budget which would then require further cuts elsewhere • Doesn't deliver forecast results • Consumes more resources which would impact other areas of the business • Customers might not respond well to new system • Employee productivity drops during changeover

When you complete a SWOT analysis consider:

- **Strengths** – these are the positive factors present in your organisation which will help the project be successful.
- **Weaknesses** – these are the negative factors which might be present in your organisation that could prevent the project from being successful.
- **Opportunities** – these are the new opportunities which the project might bring to your organisation.
- **Threats** – these are the risks which the project could bring to your organisation.

Stephen Covey's prioritisation matrix

'The key is not to prioritise what's on your schedule, but to schedule your priorities'

—Stephen Covey

A great tool to learn as you develop decision-making skills comes from Stephen Covey's best-selling book *The Seven Habits of Highly Successful People.*

The prioritisation matrix is designed to help you decide how to prioritise your time. This is a critical element of decision-making because you need to be able to determine if the task or problem you are trying to solve is worthy of your time right here and now.

The prioritisation matrix works like this. When a task comes to your attention evaluate it using two different criteria:

1. Is it urgent? – **Urgency** refers to the timeframe. When is this thing due? Does it have to be done within the next five minutes or is it due in the next month?

2. Is it important? **Importance** refers to impact. What is the impact to the organisation of completing this task? What is the negative impact if I don't complete it?

Once you have defined both criteria you are then in a position to assign it to one of the quadrants in the prioritisation matrix (see Figure 7.5).

Figure 7.5 – Stephen Covey's prioritisation matrix

	Important but not urgent *Decide when you will do it*	**Urgent and important** *Do it immediately*
IMPORTANT	**Not important, not urgent** *Do it later*	**Urgent but not important** *Delegate to someone else*

URGENT

Tasks which are highly urgent and highly important leave you with no choice than to act on them immediately.

Tasks which are highly urgent but not important can be delegated to someone else to perform so you don't fill your schedule with taks that are more appropriate for someone else to complete.

Tasks that are not urgent and not important can be left alone and you can come back to them when you have more capacity.

Tasks that are important but not urgent can be scheduled in to your workflow so that you can plan and attend to them before they become urgent.

The crossroads model

The crossroads model provides some options to consider when you find yourself at a crossroads in life with no prescribed path to choose. This model can help you set off on a completely new path or choose to follow a path you are familiar with. The model is adapted from *The Decision Book*, by Mikael Krogerus and Roman Tschappeler.[10]

The crossroads model is a useful tool for self-reflection. First of all you need to take a moment to consider and reflect on where you are today so that you can make a decision about which path you will take towards tomorrow.

Where are you today?

- What big decisions have got you to this point?
- What do you enjoy doing?
- What would you like to do more of?
- What is most important to you?
- What is holding you back from doing something you have always wanted to do?
- What are you afraid of?

Then you have to consider which path is the next one for you to choose. Is it:

- The road that beckons you – which you have always wanted to try?
- The road that you have dreamed of following?
- The road which seems most sensible to other people?
- The road not travelled yet – one you have never considered before?
- The road you have already been down?
- The road back to a safe place?

The first part of the model helps you to try to identify what is important to you and the second part provides some options to help you feel confident to make the best decision for you and your circumstances.

HOW AND WHEN TO INVOLVE YOUR TEAM IN DECISION-MAKING

As a leader you will often identify the importance of having your team engaged and aligned with a strategic direction.

One of the key ingredients in engagement is to involve your team in the decision-making process. This is particularly important if the decision will impact your team and you need their support to facilitate the solution successfully.

There are levels of involvement and delegating decision-making authority options available to you and your team:

- You make the decision and then inform your team.
- You ask the team for ideas and you make the final decision.
- You ask the team for ideas and you all make the decisions together.
- You allow the team to make the decision and inform you afterwards.

You need to weigh up the risk of your team making the wrong decision against the benefits of the team taking ownership, and decide what level of decision-making authority to give to your team.

If you do decide to get your team involved in the decision-making process you will need to decide how your group should work together to make the decision. Below are several formats for group decision-making.

Consensus

In a consensus, each person agrees to support the decision. Team members might have differing perspectives but they all agree that they can live with the decision. Consensus decision-making is likely to have the highest level of team commitment, although it can be the longest way to make a decision because all varying opinions need to be heard and discussed.

Majority rules

Majority rule decisions are made when more than half the group wants a particular outcome. This can be an efficient decision-making method because it can be conducted with a simple vote or show of hands. A potential negative to this method is that there may be several members of the group who strongly disagree and therefore will not commit to supporting the decision.

Subcommittee

A subcommittee can be formed to make a decision on behalf of a group. Usually subcommittee members have a particular interest in the outcome of the decision so they will investigate and collaborate to ensure the best outcome is met. While forming a subcommittee is a good way to make a decision without consuming the whole group there is still the potential for negativity if members of the wider group disagree with the subcommittee.

Specialist

You can refer a decision to a specialist or subject matter expert within the team and engage them to make the best decision on behalf of the whole group. This method is particularly useful if your team doesn't have the level of experience or appropriate skills to make a good decision. A potential negative is that you might not get the initial support from the rest of the group because they have been left out of the decision.

Case study: Decisiveness in the battlefield

Imagine a wartime scenario where you are under fire and surrounded by enemy soldiers. There are bullets whistling past you as you lie flat on the ground, cursing the buttons on your jacket because they elevate your body slightly, wondering how to save your forward platoon.

That was the situation Captain Greg Vivian Gilbert experienced in Vietnam on 21 September 1971.

His description of the barrage of fire, bullets coming from everywhere, scraping the dirt to get his body just a little lower, is chilling.

The forward platoon ordered to redeploy had started down a track and come up against a bunker system. They found themselves in close contact with the enemy. It was the era of air strikes with bombs and napalm; the enemy did not view them kindly. In the lead up to the incident one of his comrades had been decapitated by a rocket propelled grenade striking a tree beside him. The enemy, the North Vietnamese army, had been subjected to air strikes all day, and in the late afternoon the company mounted an attack on the bunker system which failed. Withdrawing from the bunker system, the Company moved in single file to get away from the bunkers. They could hear that the enemy had moved from the bunkers and were following them.

As luck would have it, as they withdrew they ran up against the North Vietnamese reserve bunker system. The company quickly formed a defensive circle and, soon after, as it became inky black under the jungle canopy, the enemy attacked. Captain Gilbert attempted to call to the Company Commander to coordinate an artillery response, but the enemy was close enough to shoot at him when he spoke. Captain Gilbert realised that the only possible way the Company was going to survive, surrounded as they were by the North Vietnamese, was to call in artillery fire as quickly as possible. However, he was aware that if he spoke to the Company Commander he would give their positions away, endangering their lives. It was too big a risk to take. There was uncertainty as to where they were on the map and he couldn't confirm their position without turning on his torch thus giving his position away and endangering them further. His Company Commander trusted him, and there was little opportunity for any discourse throughout the night. Captain Gilbert was on his own in calling the shots, with only his experience and skills to make decisions that would mean life or death for himself and the Company.

The Company had orders not to move out of artillery range, but they had strayed out of range of three of the six guns supporting them so there were only three guns, and they were at extreme range. At extreme range the dispersion of artillery fire can be great so there would be a danger, if Captain Gilbert got it wrong, of the artillery falling on his own troops with devastating consequences.

Captain Gilbert describes how it was pitch black, he couldn't see his map and without his compass he had to calculate their co-ordinates in his head using only trigonometry and a basic measurement that was second nature to him, paces.

He was required to make decisions in this data deprived condition contemporaneously with an emotional and physical onslaught of overwhelming proportion.

When he gave the first co-ordinates to the artillery, he could only hope they were correct. Everyone's survival depended on them. Throughout the course of the night he brought the artillery fire in closer, until it was no longer safe to do so. He did this drawing on his experience, by calculating the distance it was falling from the differentiation of the sound, and whether it was live shrapnel or dead shrapnel. He described it as a boom versus a crack. His experience also extended to having been under fire before, and not panicking; from staying calm and being able to recall trigonometry to calculate the co-ordinates in his head under extremely difficult circumstances. He understood the technical aspects of the situation;

he then incorporated evidenced-based, here and now logistics of the situation into his decision-making and acted decisively.

Around 9.00 pm firing by the North Vietnamese Army ceased. At this point Captain Gilbert issued the command to reduce firing to sporadic rather than cease completely. This strategic move maintained a presence and let the enemy know they were still ready. At dawn, expecting an attack, the company was relieved to find the enemy had withdrawn, taking their significant casualties with them.

Belatedly in 2018, after a reappraisal of the medal awards system during the Vietnam War, Captain Gilbert was awarded the Distinguished Service Medal for Leadership in Warlike Operations for his actions.

Under conditions like this, what determines leadership?

Captain Gilbert only had limited resources and data available to him, which he utilised despite it requiring a leap of faith, particularly with the first artillery when he gave the co-ordinates. Not acting would have most certainly resulted in their death. He described the process as 'I clicked into action, knew I had to do it, everyone depended on me'.

The current business environment has been likened to the US Army War College description of battlefield operations, described by the well-known acronym – VUCA:

- **Volatility** – The speed, magnitude and dynamics of change.
- **Uncertainty** – The unpredictability of issues and events.
- **Complexity** – The range and interconnectedness of issues and the chaos that surround any organisation.
- **Ambiguity** – The inability to clarify reality and decipher the mixed meanings of conditions.

Today's leaders struggle with how to lead well in a VUCA world, when old rules do not apply. Instead, connections with and between people are as important or more important than solid structures. Boundaries around organisations are less defined and no longer static, resulting in global networks of complex stakeholder relationships. There's no one button to press to create and sustain organisational success.[11]

It is all the more important in this environment that leaders are decisive.

DECISIVE LEADERSHIP

War and other crisis situations provide fresh insights into the role that leaders should play in time-sensitive, high-risk, uncertain and make-or-break situations. Although the details may differ, challenges of crisis situations resemble those frequently confronted by senior executives in today's turbulent business environment. Organisations must face and deal with threats to their prosperity and even survival in situations where risks are ineffectively understood and countermeasures are unclear. On occasions, even opportunities are difficult to decipher. Despite experience being a valuable asset and not to be undermined, the past provides little guidance on what may work in the future. Hence leaders must learn rapidly and execute reliably under rigid time constraints. A combination of these factors can result in chaotic situations, which in turn can become discouraging and even frightening. In such emotionally charged situations, leaders can feel undecided, vacillating between whether they should be directive, taking charge and monitoring people or whether to be empowering, inviting innovative ideas and experimentation.

Research has suggested that the choice presents a false dichotomy, and that both paths should be explored.[12] In complex and rapidly evolving situations leaders have to command action so that they can act efficiently and decisively to capitalise on even short-lived opportunities. Simultaneously they need to evolve with the changing landscape and stay ahead of competition.

There has been considerable debate over the power and perils of intuition. While Kahneman's Prospect Theory[13] helps explain the sometimes counter-intuitive choices people make under uncertainty, Klein has focused on the power of intuition to support good decision-making in high-pressure environments, such as firefighting and intensive-care units.[14] However, they both agree that the premortem technique, a sneaky method to engage people in contrarian devil's advocate thinking, demonstrates a leader's intelligence. By engaging the corporate culture into a competition using this premortem technique, a leader can change the whole dynamic from trying to avoid anything that might disrupt harmony to trying to surface potential problems.

As decision-making and decisiveness are fundamental to the effectiveness of leaders and axiomatically to the success of their organisations, how leaders can maximise their success rate has been examined in depth, and it has been suggested that viewing the decision as a process and not as an event is crucial.[15]

Seven steps to decisive leadership

1. **Gathering information from a broad range of sources.**
   A decisive leader avoids an echo chamber of their own opinions and instead strives to consider thoughts that differ from their own.

2. **Fostering constructive conflict.** Such conflict is best described in the context of collaborative problem-solving. The leader should encourage the sharing of information in raw form to allow others to formulate their own conclusions. This part of the process should ideally be viewed as a collective effort to test and evaluate possible alternatives to allow innovative thought to be expressed.

3. **Honestly considering the alternatives.** The act of considering the alternatives results in a leader engaging in thoughtful analysis and avoiding settling prematurely on easy, obvious answers. Any

stakeholders should feel that they had a genuine opportunity to influence the outcome; the leader should seek to achieve this by actively listening to and investigating the alternative idea presented.

4. **Not dominating the process.** The leader should avoid disclosing their personal preferences too early in the process or giving any indication they have already made a decision, so as to avoid side-tracking the process.

5. **Testing assumptions.** The leader must be able to discern between 'facts' that have been tested and those that have been merely assumed or asserted. He/she should seek the objective input of a helpful contrarian who will ask hard questions to initiate healthy debate. After the decision is made, the leader should be open to fine tuning in the event the assumptions are found to be incorrect.

6. **Making a clear yes/no decision and thoroughly explaining it.** Making a good decision loses meaning if it is not acted upon. To give credence to a decision and effectively mobilise the people and resources required to put the decision into practice, the leader must clearly explain the thought processes behind the call and convey how each participant's input affected the final decision. As different people process messages differently, the leader should be concise and avoid ambiguity in his communications.

7. **Staying involved with the execution.** If a decision is not successfully executed it is a poor decision, regardless of the thought and process behind it. Rather than simply 'pulling the trigger' a decisive leader remains engaged with the execution of the decision, requires continuous feedback on the results, makes adjustments if necessary and provides active support to those whose remit it is to carry out the decision.

Certain habits have been discovered to be associated with making bad decisions. They are laziness, not anticipating unexpected events (failure to consider from a negative event perspective), indecisiveness (considering the data in depth but failing to move forward and make the decision), remaining locked in the past (relying on approaches that worked in the past and not considering alternative methods in a changing environment), having no strategic alignment (failure to connect the problem to the overall strategy, an absence of context), over-dependence (not acting independently when required), isolation (failure to involve others with relevant knowledge and skill), lack of technical depth (failure to have or gain a perspective of their own in required areas of expertise), failure to communicate (not actually communicating the decision or implementing it).[16]

In a real-world scenario, leaders must make decisions at the speed of business. Effective leaders deal with ambiguity every day and must learn to decide and act without always having the complete picture. Speed of decision-making becomes of the essence in terms of a leader being viewed as decisive.

Three other factors have been found to impact on becoming a decisive leader.[17]

1. **Reflective urgency.** This is the ability to consciously and rapidly reflect on the priorities, resources and needs of the moment. Such a technique requires developing and maintaining a balanced big picture view of the business as an entity, which in turn requires being constantly aware of the most important near-term priorities and balancing them with their long-term impact and the resources available in the moment. In essence, reflective urgency can be regarded as a form of integrated thinking, where two conflicting ideas are held and explored at the same time; using this strategy the leader will discover the path to the most important priority of the moment.

2. **Determination of personal data threshold for the leader.**
   While the temptation may be to gather information until
   100% of available data is at hand before contemplating
   making a decision, in reality leaders will never be able
   to access all of the information available. Attempting to
   gather information of such depth and breadth will bring the
   decision-making process to a halt, paralysing the leader and
   axiomatically the organisation. Therefore, leaders should
   instead find a comfort zone for their 'data threshold', which
   will help them identify the direction and magnitude of the
   decision at hand and to weigh the most salient facts.

3. **Remembering that a wrong decision is better than no
   decision at all.** This is the realisation that there are few decisions in business or life that cannot be reversed or modified.
   Notwithstanding that outcomes matter, it must be kept in
   mind that it is rare that they are permanent. A good leader
   will inevitably make a wrong decision at some juncture. This
   realisation is incredibly liberating and enables leaders to
   make decisions more rapidly and keep things in perspective.
   Wrong decisions can be fixed but indecisiveness will damage
   a leader's reputation and organisation beyond repair.

Business is a contact sport; a leader can't be afraid to make a mistake. While the decision can always be revised, and the course
corrected, a leader cannot make up for failing to take action when
it was required and risking missing the opportunity completely.[18]

Decision-making is a process and although it can be enhanced
by information gathering and honest consideration of the
alternatives, and testing the assumptions, there are times when
the speed of business dictates the speed of decision-making.

This is when reflective urgency and making a decision instead of lengthy procrastinating are required.

Indecisiveness has been described as the kiss of death for leaders. Yukio Hatoyama, Japan's Prime Minister, gained a reputation for being indecisive and lost the faith of his voters and party.[19]

As the pace of change increases, a leader's ability to make high quality decisions quickly and accurately is going to prove increasingly more critical. Bad decisions can place organisations in jeopardy, but delayed decisions can cost through loss of a competitive advantage. Leaders need to be competent at looking at the facts, discussing the options and making a decision. Being decisive involves making decisions and continually moving forward, even in an environment of uncertainty, balancing reflection with decisiveness, and making good decisions based on a mixture of analysis, wisdom, experience and judgement.

Research has noted eight factors which enabled leaders to be more decisive. They are:

1. **Risk taking** – it is essential for leaders to analyse data, examine trends and anticipate problems if 'analysis paralysis' indecisiveness develops. Eventually they need to take a risk and make a decision.

2. **Communicating powerfully** – a decisive leader continually keeps others informed. Being effective at sharing information often results in others raising pertinent questions and challenging assumptions.

3. **Having a strategic perspective** – many decisions can actually result in a temporary dip in performance; thus, it is essential for a leader to take a strategic long-term view to assist in making a good decision fit into the longer term

strategy of the organisation. Without the long view leaders often steer away from a good decision that could result in significant competitive advantage.

4. **Seeking technical expertise** – evaluation can be impeded when a leader is technologically over their head. Effective leaders involve others who have the requisite expertise despite it requiring humility on their part.

5. **Courage** – while others may have contributed to a decision, leaders need to be willing to be accountable. It is a moment that requires courage and ability to stand alone.

6. **Driving for results** – when a decision is made it must be followed through and implemented quickly by the leader, effectively giving it a 'push' failing which it won't be a successful decision.

7. **Being inspiring** – for decisions to be successfully implemented there needs to be a 'pull'. Leaders need the ability to inspire and energise others.

8. **Having integrity** – leaders who possess a strong sense of integrity are able to be more decisive. Asking the question 'What is the right thing to do?' simplifies the decision-making process.

Striving towards improvement in these behaviours will have a profound positive impact on a leader's ability to be decisive.[20]

EMOTIONAL INTELLIGENCE AND DECISION-MAKING UNDER PRESSURE

As a leader you will be faced with situations where you are required to make a decision in difficult conditions. It could be that there is time pressure, high risk or it's a highly emotive topic that you need to act on. Emotional intelligence refers to your ability to understand your emotional reaction to a situation and to manage your response appropriately. It also refers to your ability to recognise and understand the emotional responses of those around you.

To make a good decision you need to utilise your emotional intelligence to understand which emotions are useful to the decision and which are clouding your judgement. You will need a clear frame of mind to understand the facts of the situation and to weigh up your options. You also have to recognise if your colleagues are in the right emotional frame to make or implement a good decision.

Emotions may include:

- Being excited about achieving a particular outcome.
- Fear of making a mistake.
- Anger at a situation or problem, which has occurred out of your control.

Any emotion has the ability to cloud your judgement and prevent you from making a decision. Leaders should learn to identify what emotion they are feeling and determine whether it is useful or a hindrance to the decision at hand. If the emotion is too strong to be managed a leader needs to defer the decision until later or potentially use a colleague as a sounding board to help sense check any ideas.

REDUCING RISK IN DECISION-MAKING

As a leader you want to feel confident that you have made the right decision and often you won't know if it's the right decision until after it has been implemented. Most leaders don't want to make the wrong decision that will flow on to have a negative impact through their organisation. To help you manage this uncertainty you can use some basic risk management principles as part of your decision-making process.

Firstly, you need to brainstorm all the reasons why your decision might be unsuccessful. For example:

- The staff won't like it.
- The staff won't be able to learn the new system.
- The budget might get cut.

Then you need to assess two factors against each of your reasons:

1. How likely is it to occur?
2. What are the consequences if it does?

Then you can work out the riskiness of the decision using the matrix in Figure 7.6 below.

Figure 7.6 – The risk matrix

LIKELIHOOD				
	Likely	Medium risk	High risk	Extreme risk
	Unlikely	Low risk	Medium risk	High risk
	Highly unlikely	Insignificant risk	Low risk	Medium risk
		Slightly harmful	Harmful	Extremely harmful

CONSEQUENCES

This will help you to determine if the risks are genuine and need further actions. You might decide that the potential consequences are too significant and so the option is not appropriate. Alternatively, you might decide that the risk is not all that bad and so you might decide to proceed.

THE FINAL WORD ON DECISIVENESS

Making decisions is a core part of a leader's role. Your team and your organisation are relying on you to make the best decision aligned with your organisation's vision, values and strategy. You will need to work through your emotions and gather the relevant facts so that you can make the best possible decision at that time.

You need to consider how important the decision is to your team and make a judgement about getting them involved in the decsion if necessary.

Above all, remember that leadership is a learning journey and we should invest time in learning from our successes and our failures so that we can continue to grow.

'A peacefulness follows any decision, even the wrong ones'.
—Rita Mae Brown

LEAD WELL. GO CHARTERED!

I won't lie; the shift from being inspired by *leadership* rather than individual leaders is an incredibly difficult change in thinking. It's one that involves understanding exactly what makes leaders good at what they do. It's something that this book sets out to help you with by focusing on seven key leadership attributes: respect, integrity, emotional intelligence, ability to inspire, authenticity, self-awareness and decisiveness.

As the Chair of the Board of the largest leadership body across Australia and New Zealand – one that passionately believes that leaders are made and not born – I've spent most of my life attempting to understand how good leaders lead well. I have worked for and studied many good leaders who not only possess sound practical skills but also crucial leadership attributes.

Many people I've encountered throughout my career have shaped themselves in the image of the leaders they're inspired by. These have often been CEOs of large multinationals, world leaders or successful entrepreneurs. They've benchmarked their success against the personal and professional experiences of these individuals, adopting both the good and bad traits of these leaders.

While this can be useful in developing your leadership skills and charting a course on your own leadership journey, it can also be problematic; you are not them! The leaders that we seek to mirror and imitate have their own experiences, backgrounds, histories and genes that form the basis of their leadership actions and styles. Benchmarking our leadership heroes will only take us so far.

That isn't to say that benchmarking sound leadership practice is a bad thing. A benchmark that is objective and impassive and that represents gold standard leadership can be a real game-changer in the life – and career – of a leader, *which is why Chartered Manager is so significant.*

Chartered Manager is the global highest status that can be achieved as a manager and leader. Recognised by Royal Charter, this prestigious professional designation accredits management and leadership excellence.

The Institute of Managers and Leaders (IML) introduced Chartered Manager to Australia and New Zealand in 2017 in the absence of a satisfactory benchmark for leadership. Research reports from the last two decades consistently revealed a systematic failure of leadership in our organisations with no tangible mark of good leadership to achieve. After seeing its international success, we forged a strategic partnership with the Chartered Management Institute in the UK to bring the Chartered Manager accreditation to Australia and New Zealand.

Focused on continuing professional development (CPD), the chartership requires leaders to prove their experience and knowledge, and to commit to future growth in leadership practice. The assessment and CPD are underpinned by a skills-focused framework of 34 practical leadership competencies that covers everything from managing conflict to promoting equality of opportunity, diversity and inclusion. This ensures Chartered professionals have the hands-on skills to lead people effectively and successfully.

Most significant, is the fact that the accreditation is built on four key pillars:

1. Knowledge and expertise
2. Practical difference to the workplace
3. Continuing professional development
4. Ethical practice.

These four pillars represent the fundamental groundwork of leadership. They are the attributes aspiring leaders should aim to have in order to be successful.

To me, Chartered Manager is the epitome of the crucial balance of leadership inspiration and perspiration – both the correct skills and the mindset of a great leader. As an accreditation, Chartered Manager isn't about good leaders, it's about good leadership, and thus, it is the benchmark we should use to develop it.

In so many professions around the world – be it engineering or accounting or law – professional designations are required that certify someone has the essential knowledge and demonstrable skills to carry out their role effectively and with the utmost integrity. Accreditation represents the highest standard, and Chartered Manager, like other designations, ensures professionals are being developed to that level.

On an individual level, managers seek to professionalise their leadership experience and gain a competitive edge in the market. For organisations developing their staff, the tangible leadership benchmark dramatically lifts employee engagement, retention and business success. For universities increasing the employability of their graduates, putting students on the pathway to achieving the globally-recognised accreditation provides a clear roadmap to good leadership.

Leading well starts with the right leadership inspiration.

Start your leadership journey with Chartered Manager. Or, as we say at the Institute: Go Chartered!

If you want to get accredited with the global highest status of management and leadership:

    call: **1300 661 061**
    email: **chartered.manager@managersandleaders.com.au**

To find out more about Chartered Manager:

    visit: **www.charteredmanager.com.au**

Ann Messenger
Chair, Institute of Managers and Leaders

REFERENCES

Chapter 1

1. SHRM, 2017. *Employee Job Satisfaction and Engagement: The Doors of Opportunity Are Open*, Society for Human Resource Management, https://www.shrm.org/hr-today/trends-and-forecasting/research-and-surveys/pages/2017-job-satisfaction-and-engagement-doors-of-opportunity-are-open.aspx

Chapter 2

1. http://www.roymorgan.com/findings/7244-roy-morgan-image-of-professions-may-2017-201706051543
2. Ariely, D. (2012) 'Why we lie', *Wall Street Journal*, 26 May 2012, https://www.wsj.com/articles/SB10001424052702304840904577422090013997320?mod=wsj_share_tweet&mg=reno64-wsj&url=http%253A%252F%252Fonline.wsj.com%252
3. Kranhold, K., Lee, B. and Benson, M. (2012) 'New Documents Show Enron Traders Manipulated California Energy Costs', *Wall Street Journal*, 7 May 2012, http://www.wsj.com/articles/SB1020718637382274400
4. *Time* (2007) 'The worst cars of all time', *Time*, http://content.time.com/time/specials/2007/article/0,28804,1658545_1658498_1657866,00.html
5. Festinger, L. (1957) *A theory of cognitive dissonance*, Stanford, Stanford University Press
6. Brenner, M. (1996) 'The man who knew too much', *Vanity Fair*, May 1996, http://www.vanityfair.com/magazine/1996/05/wigand199605
7. Salter, C. (2002) 'Jeffrey Wigand: The whistle blower', *Fast Company*, 30 April 2002, http://www.fastcompany.com/65027/jeffrey-wigand-whistle-blower
8. Chabris, C. and Simons, D. (2010) *The Invisible Gorilla*, New York, Crown Publishers
9. Kahneman, D. (2011) *Thinking, Fast and Slow*, New York, Farrar, Straus and Giroux

10. Banaji, M., Bazerman, M. and Chugh, D. (2003) 'How unethical are you?' *Harvard Business Review*, December 2003, p. 59

11. George, B. (2007) *True North: Discover your authentic leadership*, San Francisco, Jossey-Bass

12. Bigelow, K. (unknown), Quote, http://www.brainyquote.com/quotes/quotes/k/kathrynbig254781.html

13. Cleary, T. (2004) *Zen Lessons: the art of leadership*, Boston, Shambhala, p. 201

14. Soll, J., Milkman, K. and Payne, J. (2015) 'Outsmart your own biases', *Harvard Business Review*, May 2015, p.68

Chapter 3

1. Goleman, D. (2012) *Emotional Intelligence: Why It Can Matter More Than IQ*, Bantam

2. Ibid., p.16

3. CMI's Emotional Intelligence checklist 178, https://www.managers.org.uk/~/media/Files/Campus%20CMI/Checklists%20First%20Management%20Role/Emotional%20intelligence.ashx

4. https://www.genosinternational.com/workplace-behaviour/

5. Chartered Management Institute's Membership Direct database.

6. https://psychcentral.com/news/2011/10/21/iq-can-significantly-change-during-adolescence/30587.html

7. https://www.managers.org.uk/~/media/Files/Campus%20CMI/Checklists%20First%20Management%20Role/Emotional%20intelligence.ashx

8. Marsland, K. W. and Likavec, S. C. (2003) 'Maternal emotional intelligence, infant attachment and child socio-emotional competence'. Paper presented at the 15th Annual Meeting of the American Psychological Society, Atlanta, GA

9. Mayer et al, (1999) 'Emotional intelligence meets traditional standards for an intelligence', ScienceDirect, https://www.sciencedirect.com/science/article/pii/S0160289699000161

10. Goleman, D. (2000) 'Leadership that gets results', *Harvard Business Review*, March-April

11. Cherniss, C. (1999) 'The Business Case for Emotional Intelligence', RMIT, https://emedia.rmit.edu.au/leadrmit/sites/default/files/The%20Business%20Case%20for%20Emotional%20Intelligence.pdf

12. Dudley, G.W. and Goodson, S.L. (2001) 'Sales call reluctance among Americans, Australians and New Zealanders'
13. Voss, C. (2017) *Never split the difference – Negotiating as if your life depended on it*, Cornerstone, UK

Chapter 4

1. Kouzes, J.M. and Posner, B.Z. (2002) *The Leadership Challenge*, John Wiley & Sons
2. Levin, M. (2017) 'Why Great Leaders (Like Richard Branson) Inspire Instead of Motivate', *Inc.*, https://www.inc.com/marissa-levin/why-great-leaders-like-richard-branson-inspire-instead-of-motivate.html
3. Eichenwald, M. (2017) 'The Importance of inspirational Leadership', *Chief Learning Officer*, February, http://www.clomedia.com/2017/02/27/importance-inspirational-leadership-reshaped-world/
4. The HOW Report (2016) 'A Global Empirical Analysis of How Governance, Culture and Leadership Impact Performance'
5. Steffens, K. N. and Haslam, S. A. (2013) 'Power through "us": Leaders' use of we-referencing language predicts election victory', *PloS ONE*, 8(10): e77952
6. Molenberghs, P., Prochilo, G., Steffens, N.K., Zacher, H. and Haslam, S.A. (2015) 'The neuroscience of inspirational leadership: The importance of collective-oriented language and shared group membership', *Journal of Management*, DOI: 10.1177/0149206314565242
7. Horowich, M. and Whipple Callahan, M. (2016) 'How Leaders Inspire: Cracking the Code', Bain Research, June 10 2016, http://www.bain.com/publications/articles/how-leaders-inspire-cracking-the-code.aspx
8. Heathfield, S. (2018) 'What Makes a Leader Inspirational to People?', The balance: careers, May 27, 2018, https://www.thebalancecareers.com/leadership-inspiration-1918611
9. Comaford (2013), as cited by Levin, 'Science Says Provide These Three Things', *Inc.*, 2016, https://www.inc.com/marissa-levin/want-to-increase-employee-loyalty-by-67-100-science-says-to-provide-these-3-thi.html
10. Holladay, S.J. and Coombs, W.T. (1993). 'Communicating visions: An exploration of the role of delivery in the creation of leader charisma', *Management Communication Quarterly*, 6(4): 405-427

11. Holladay, S.J. and Coombs, W.T. (1994) 'Speaking of visions and visions being spoken: An exploration if the effects of content and delivery and perceptions of leader charisma', *Management Communication Quarterly*, 8(2): 165-189.

12. Kirkpatrick, S.A., and Locke, E.A. (1996) 'Direct and indirect effects of three core charismatic leadership components on performance and attitudes', *Journal of Applied Psychology*, 8(1): 36-51.

13. Awamleh, R. and Gardner, W.L. (1999) 'Perceptions of Leader Charisma and effectiveness; The effects of vision, content, delivery and organizational performance', *The Leadership Quarterly*, 10,345-373.

14. Erickson, A.D. (2005) 'Charismatic rhetoric and follower effects. The mediating role of follower affect', Unpublished Doctoral Dissertation, Bond University, Australia

15. Sashkin, M. (1998) The visionary leader. In J.A. Conger and R.A. Kanungo (eds.) *Charismatic Leadership: The elusive factor in organizational effectiveness:* 122-160. San Francisco, CA: Jossey-Bass

16. Edinger, J.A., and Patterson, M.L. 'Non-verbal involvement and social control', *Psychological Bulletin*, 1983, 93(1):30-56

17. Shamir, B., House, R.J., and Arthur, M.B. (1993) 'The motivational effects of charismatic leadership: A self-concept based theory', *Organizational Science*, 4 577-594.

18. Garton, E. (2017) 'How to be an Inspiring Leader', *Harvard Business Review*, April, https://hbr.org/2017/04/how-to-be-an-inspiring-leader

Chapter 5

1. Sandberg, S. (2013) *Lean In: women, work and the will to lead*, Random House, New York

2. McLeod, S. (2013) 'Pavlov's Dogs', Simplypsychology.org, http://www.simplypsychology.org/pavlov.html.

3. I first became aware of this concept through the work of Human Synergistics International and undergoing 360-degree feedback using their *Life Styles Inventory*™ survey and *Leadership Impact*® survey

4. Edelman, S. (2006) *Change Your Thinking*, 2nd Ed, ABC Books

5. Grant, A. M. (2016) *Originals: How Non-conformists Change the World*, Random House

6. The conscious competence model is cited as being developed by Gordon Training International. Their website states 'This Learning Stages model was developed by former GTI employee, Noel Burch over 30 years ago'. http://www.gordontraining.com/free-workplace-articles/learning-a-new-skill-is-easier-said-than-done/

7. http://www.wordsfitlyspoken.org/gospel_guardian/v20/v20n41p1-3a.html

8. Brown, B. (2012) *Daring Greatly: How the Courage to Be Vulnerable Transforms the Way We Live, Love, Parent and Lead*, Penguin

9. Brown, B. (2010) *The Gifts of Imperfection: Let Go of Who You Think You're Supposed to Be and Embrace Who You Are*, Hazeldon

10. Brown, B. (2016) My response to Adam Grant's *New York Times* Op/ED: Unless You're Oprah, 'Be Yourself' Is Terrible Advice, https://www.linkedin.com/pulse/my-response-adam-grants-new-york-times-oped-unless-youre-bren%C3%A9-brown/?trk=aff_src.aff-lilpar_c.partners_learning&irgwc=1

11. Krieg, G. (May 2018) *How can Trump lie so much and be authentic at the same time?* CNN Politics, https://edition.cnn.com/2018/05/05/politics/trumps-lies-authentic-to-his-supporters/index.html

12. Baldoni, J. (January 2016) 'Is Donald Trump a role model for authenticity?', *Forbes*, https://www.forbes.com/sites/johnbaldoni/2016/01/02/is-donald-trump-a-role-model-for-authenticity/#33bed66a33bc

13. Hill, A. (February 2017) 'Trump's plain speaking fuels the leadership cult of authenticity', *Financial Times*, https://www.ft.com/content/f168807e-e8a8-11e6-893c-082c54a7f539

14. Kenny, C. (June 2018) 'No Filter Trump makes a great communicator', *The Australian*, https://www.theaustralian.com.au/news/inquirer/straight-talk-from-trump-spin-time-for-the-media/news-story/c8d70da6255b507034fdf5cd10fd6000

15. Tanner, C. (May 2018) 'Study finds Trump voters believe Trump is authentic, even if he appears to lie', *USA Today*, https://www.usatoday.com/story/news/politics/onpolitics/2018/05/02/trump-supporters-were-more-enthusiastic-their-support-him-candidate-extent-they-justified-trumps-lie/573371002/

16. George, B. (2003) *Authentic Leadership: Rediscovering the Secrets to Creating Lasting Value*, Jossey-Bass, San Francisco

Chapter 6

1. EBSCO (2010) 'You don't have to say you love me', referencing: Dozier, J. (2010) *The Weeping, the Window, the Way*, Tate Publishing
2. Somers, M. (2009) *Instant Manager: Coaching*, [CMI] Hodder & Stoughton
3. http://fortune.com/2015/04/02/quit-reasons/
4. Senge, Peter M. (2006) *The Fifth Discipline*, Bantam Doubleday Dell Publishing Group
5. Somers, M. Op. cit.

Chapter 7

1. Carucci, R. (2018) 'Leaders, Stop Avoiding Avoiding Hard Questions', *Harvard Business Review*, https://hbr.org/2018/04/leaders-stop-avoiding-hard-decisions
2. Van Wart, M. and Kapucu, N. (2011) 'Crisis Management Competencies', *Public Management Review*, 2011, 13:4, 489-511
3. Floyd, D.L., Prentice-Dunn, S. and Rogers, R.W. (2000) 'A Meta Analysis of Research on Protection Motivation Theory', *Journal of Applied Social Psychology*, 2000, Vol.30(2), 407-429
4. Mann, L., Burnett, P., Radford, M. and Ford, S. (1997) 'The Melbourne Decision Making Questionnaire: An Instrument for Measuring Patterns for Coping with Decisional Conflict', *Journal of Behavioural Decision Making*, 1997, Vol.10, 1-19
5. Colakkadioglu, O. and Gucray, S.S. (2012) 'The Effect of Conflict Theory Based Decision-Making Skill Training Psycho-Educational Group Experience on Decision Making Styles of Adolescents', *Educational Sciences: Theory and Practice*, 12(2) 669-676
6. Mann, L., Beswick, G., Allouache, P. and Ivey, M. (1989) 'Decision Workshops for the Improvement of Decision-Making Skills and Confidence', *Journal of Counseling and Development*, 1989, Vol. 67, Issue 8, p478
7. House, R.J., Filley, A. and Gujarati, D.N. (1971) 'Leadership style, hierarchical influence, and the satisfaction of subordinate role expectations: A test of Likert's influence proposition', *Journal of Applied Psychology*, 1971, Vol 55 (5), 422-432

8. Myers, C. (2017) 'How To Become A More Decisive Leader', *Forbes*, April 2017, https://www.forbes.com/sites/chrismyers/2017/04/28/how-to-become-a-more-decisive-leader/#6a92dc417433

9. Gibson, M. and Weber, R.J. (2015) 'Applying Leadership Qualities of Great People to your Department: Sir Winston Churchill', *Hosp Pharm*, 2015, 50(1): 78-83

10. Krogerus, M. and Tschappeler, R. (2017) *The Decision Book*, Profile Books

11. Morin, T. (2008) *Characteristics of Effective Leadership*, WJM Associates

12. Horney, N. Pasmore, B. and O'Shea, T. (2010) 'Leadership Agility: A Business Imperative for a VUCA World', *People and Strategy*, vol. 33, no. 4, pp. 32-38

13. Kahneman, D. and Klein, G. (2010) 'Strategic decisions: When can you trust your gut?', *McKinsey Quarterly*, March 2010, https://www.mckinsey.com/business-functions/strategy-and-corporate-finance/our-insights/strategic-decisions-when-can-you-trust-your-gut

14. Klein G. (2007) 'Performing a Project Premortem', *Harvard Business Review*, hbr.org/2007/09/performing-a-project-premortem

15. Morin, T. Op. cit.

16. Infographic: *9 Habits That Lead To Terrible Decision-Making*, Zenger Folkman, Jan 7, 2015, http://zengerfolkman.com/infographic-9-habits-that-lead-to-terrible-decision-making/

17. Myers, C. Op. cit.

18. Whittaker, J. (2013) Instant MBA: The Most Important Trait A Leader Can Have Is Decisiveness, *Business Insider*, June 2013, https://www.businessinsider.com/most-important-trait-a-leader-can-have-is-decisiveness-2013-6?r=US&IR=T

19. McKee, J. (2010) 'Indecisiveness is the kiss of death for leaders', *Tech Decision Maker*, https://www.techrepublic.com/blog/tech-decision-maker/indecisiveness-is-the-kiss-of-death-for-leaders/

20. Folkman, J. (2017) 'Your Indecision is Costing Too much! 8 Proven Behaviours To Help You Be More decisive', *Forbes*, https://www.forbes.com/sites/joefolkman/2017/10/05/your-indecision-is-costing-too-much-8-proven-behaviors-to-become-more-decisive/#2d432bb53755

INDEX

#metoo movement 161
100 Women of Influence 186
20th century leaders and 21st century employees 108-110
21st century workplace leaders 126
360-degree feedback 72, 87, 88, 118, 153, 210, 211-212

ability to inspire 97-126
achievement, recognising 110
ALH Group 160-161
alignment 131-133, 136
analysis 41
analytics 210
anchoring 44, 45
aptitude 41-42, 52-53
Ariely, Dan Dr 32
Atlassian Corporation 112
Australian Banking Royal Commission 160
anthentic, costs of not being 133-135
authentic leadership 170, 175-176, 202
authentic organisations 158-159, 162
authenticity 7, 19, 67, 95, 127-164, 187
– barriers to 145-147
– the dark side 156-157
awareness 41, 42-43
– of others 67, 95

Bain Research 108
banking sector 35
BarOn Emotional Quotient Inventory 83
Batson, Daniel 54
Battista, Orlando A. 52
behaviour, changing 139, 147-149, 216
Behrendt, Susanne 59, 60
BeyondBlue 168
bias 40, 42
– structuring out your 56-58
– triggers 50-51
Bigelow, Kathryn 49
Bin Laden, Osama 113
blind spots 42, 176, 189, 196, 204, 206
brains 43-44, 178, 179
Branson, Richard 1, 53, 113, 235
Brexit 21-22
Broadwell, Martin M. 151
Brown, Brené 152
Buchanan, John 173-176
Buddha 29
burnout syndrome 95
Business Case for Emotional Intelligence, The 81
business outcomes 4
busyness 54

Cadbury Schweppes 26, 27
Cairns, Gordon 161

Cambridge University 177
Cannon-Brookes, Mike 112
CanTeen 22, 128
capability, developing 149
Career Leap 30
Castro, Fidel 46
CEO Genome project 172
Chabris, Christopher 39
challenging the status quo 100
Challenor, Luke 227, 228
Change your Thinking 146
charismatic leader 130
chartered accountant 60, 61
Chartered Management Institute
    (CMI) 69
Chartered Manager 261, 262, 263
Cherniss, Cary 81
Churchill, Winston 235-236
Classic Conditioning 144
Clinton, Bill 113
CMI's EI Indicator 68-70
coaching culture 219
cognitive bias 44-47
Collins, Jim 105
Comaford, Christine 111
command and control leadership
    9, 12
communicating 7, 11, 77, 78, 79,
    111, 113, 170
Competency Model of Emotional
    Intelligence 79-80
conflict theory 234
consciousness 36
consensus decision-making 247
consistent leadership 117
continuing professional
    development 262

continuous improvement 110
control and responsibility 116
corporate values
courage 36, 155, 257
Covey, Stephen 223, 243
creative thinking 77, 78
crisis management competencies
    theory 233
Critchlow, Hannah 177-183
Cuba 46
cultural change 159
culture 7, 12, 34, 35
curiosity 171
curiosity quotient (CQ) 73
customer experience 126

Daring Greatly 152
Darley, John 54
Decision Book, The 245
decision-making 32, 47, 51, 54,
    77, 78, 190-191, 197
 - avoiding 231-232
 - crossroads model 245
 - involving your team 246-248
 - models 236-240
 - pros and cons process 241
 - reducing risk in 258-259
 - theories 233
decisive leadership 251-252
 - seven steps to 252-253
decisiveness 7, 227-260
DiSC profiling 85, 196
diverse workforces 21, 23
Dr Faustus 37
Dweck, Carol 143

Edelman Trust Barometer 31

Edelman, Dr Sarah 146
Einstein, Albert vi
Emerson, Ralph Waldo 145
Emotional and Social
  Competence Inventory (ESCI)
  83
Emotional Intelligence 62
emotional intelligence 59-95, 139,
  185, 257-258
- and negotiations 92-93
- and performance management
  89-92
- and recruitment 81-86
- and sales 86-88
- competency model 72
- Development (MSCEIT-D) 85,
  86
- defining 64-68
- in the workplace 76
- learning 70-72
- maternal scores of 71
- models 71-72
- tests 83-83, 103
emotional reasoning 67, 95
emotions 174, 177-179, 184, 193
empathy 103, 207
employee engagement 101,
  117-118, 163
employee experience 12
empowering others 7
engagement 117-119
enlightenment 55
Enron 34
espoused values 33
ethical leadership 31
external assessment 82

Facebook 139, 158
faking it as a leader 202
Farquhar, Scott 112
Fearnley, Kurt 175
feedback 20, 90-91, 132, 136, 137,
  141-142, 144, 188, 205, 206, 217
Festinger, Leon 37
Financial Services Royal
  Commission 35
fixed mindset 143
Ford Pinto 34
Ford, Henry 53
Foulkes, Graham 26, 27
Foundations of Intentional
  Leadership Development
  Program 228
Four Limbs of Leadership 55
Frankl, Viktor 144
Franklin, Benjamin 39
Friedman, Thomas L. 73

Gandhi, Mahatma vi, 113, 127
Gates, Bill 53
gender bias 215
Genos 103
Genos Emotional Intelligence
  Inventory 83
Genos Emotional Intelligence
  Model 65-68
George, Bill 48, 158
Getgood, Jamie 1, 2, 9
Gibbings, Michelle 29, 30
Gilbert, Capt Greg Vivian 248-250
Glasbergen 82
GM Holden 2, 9-16
Goleman, Daniel 62, 64, 65, 79,
  80, 201

Good to Great 105
gorilla experiment 39-40
Grant, Adam 148
gratitude 27
Group Emotional Competence
   (GEC) inventory 83
growth and development 116
growth mindset 143

Habitz, Gunnar 73-76
Hallowell, Edward 94
happiness 127
Harman, Georgie 168-172
Harvard Business Review 79, 94
Harvard Business School 109
Hatoyama, Yukio 256
health professionals 31
Hitler, Adolf 113
Hochschild, Arlie 148
honesty 31
Hosseini, Khaled 53
hostage negotiator 92
HOW Report 101-102
HR manager 26, 63
Huffington, Arrianna 53
humility 7

Iacocca, Lee 113
IML 360 Analytical Tool 211-214
IML National Salary Survey 216
IML's 21st century leadership
   research 76-78
IML's Inclusion Statement 23-24
impact 133, 140
Implicit Association Test 44
indecisiveness 256
in-group bias 104

inspiration v-vi, 101, 174-175,
   180-181, 185-187, 194
– behaviours of 102
inspirational leadership within
   organisations 105-106
inspirational leadership, and the
   role of EI 103-104
inspiring yourself 119-121
Institute of Managers and Leaders
   (IML) vii, 23, 25, 210, 262
integrity 7, 29-58, 110, 111, 168,
   173, 184, 192, 257
– core attributes of 36
– strengthening 39-38
intent, sharing 140, 141

Jennings, Sue 87, 88
job satisfaction 8-9
Jobs, Steve vi, 53, 113
Johari Window model of self-
   awarenesss 204-205, 206, 207
Jung, C.G 199

Kahneman, Daniel 44
Kahneman's Prospect Theory 252
Kennedy, John F. 46
Keogh, Allison 127, 128
Kernoczy, Bill 227, 228
key performance indicators
   (KPIs) 7, 20
King, Martin Luther 113
Kite Runner, The 53
Klein, G. 253
Krogerus, Mikael 245
Kyi, Aung San Suu vii

lazy leaders 218, 223

leadership attributes vii-viii
leadership genius vi-vii
Leadership Matters v, vi, 25, 200
leading by example 7
learning from your mistakes 42, 52-53
Level 5 Leadership 105-107
Levin, Marissa 11-112, 101
listening 7, 17-18, 111, 222
loss aversion 46

management process 4, 5
management sharing information 116
managing time 77, 78, 79
Marlowe, Christopher 37
Marsten, Williams 85
Mathieson, Ian 218
Mayer, John D. 65
Mayer-Salovey-Caruso Emotional Intelligence Test (MSCEIT) 83, 103
meditation 56, 182
memory 43
meta-cognition 50
mindfulness 56
mindset, changing 149
mission 7, 111, 140
mistakes, admitting your 220
moral values 114
motivation 9, 20, 101, 103, 115-117
motivational theory 130
Musk, Elon vii
Myers Briggs 210

negotiations, relational 92, 93

negotiations, transactional 92, 93
neuroscience 104-105
Never split the difference – Negotiating as if your life depended on it 92
non-verbal behaviour 114

Obama, Barack 104
organisational performance 3
Oxford English Dictionary 5

Palmer, Dr Benjamin 65, 66, 87, 88
passion quotient (PQ) 73
Pavlov, Ivan 144
people-first 10, 12, 13, 16
performance assessment 82
performance management 90, 91, 202
personality layers 143
perspiration of leadership v-vi
Phillips, Richard 10
positive influence 68, 95
power 189-190, 196
presentation skills 202-203
Princeton University 54
prioritisation matrix 243, 244
problem-solving 77, 78, 233
professional development 209-210
protection motivation theory 233
psychometric assessments 84, 85
purpose 7, 48-49, 104, 140

recognition 117
recruitment 23
religious beliefs 22
reputation 31

resilience 76, 79
respect 1-28, 176, 196
- 5 steps to building 16-20
- complexity of 20-22
- definition of 5-6
- in the workplace 6-8
respect-based leadership 9-16
Revelian Behavioural Profile –
  Development (RBP-D) 85
rewarding 20
rhetoric 113-114
risk matrix 259
Roddick, Anita 113
role-modelling 153
Roosevelt, Theodore 59, 113, 227
Roy Morgan Image of Professions
  survey 31
Royal Flying Doctor Service 192
Rubinsztein-Dunlop, Prof Halina
  107-108

SAGE Australia 108
Salovey, Peter 65
same sex marriage debate 24-26
Sandberg, Sheryl 139
Sanofi-Aventis 87
Schultz, Howard 115
self, being your best 217-218
self-awareness 67, 82, 85, 95, 103,
  139, 171, 183, 199-226
- checklist 225
- of gender 214-216
self-esteem 114
self-management 68, 95
self-management competencies
  77, 78
self-reflection 144, 245

self-regulation 103
self-respect 16-17
servant leadership 18
setting the standard 18-19
Seven Habits of Highly Successful
  People, The 243
Sherry, Ann 184-191
Simons, Dan 39
Sinek, Simon 73, 140
situational leadership 99-100
Smith, Margot 199, 200
social awareness 103
social identity theory 104
Society of Human Resources
  Management 8
soft skills 76
Staib, Meredith 192-197
Starbucks 115
Start With Why 73
Step Up 30
stereotypes 21
Sterne, Laurence 16
strategy 7, 219, 256
Strauss, Claude Levi 58
Strayed, Cheryl 49
strengthened integrity model
  40-42
Swinburne University 65
SWOT analysis 241-243

technical expertise 257
thank you, the power of 26-28
The Gifts of Imperfection 152
theories of leadership 99
theory of cognitive dissonance 37
theory of consciousness 204
Thinking, Fast and Slow 44

threat appraisal process 234
Trait Emotional Intelligence
  Questionnaire (TEIQue) 83
transactional leadership 99-100
transformational leadership
  99-100, 131-132
transition 13, 14-15
transparency 14, 162
True North 48
Trump, Donald 156
trust 7, 14, 31, 111, 169
Tuckman's team development
  model 123-125
Turnbull Government 24

unconscious bias 108
unconscious competence cycle
  151
understanding 22

values 140, 162
values system 111
vision 4, 7, 111, 113, 158
voluntary work 208-209
von Moltke, General Helmuth 218
Voss, Chris 92
vulnerability 152, 171

Wang, Vera 53
Weinstein, Harvey 161
Welch, Jack 97
Wigand, Jeffrey 38
Wild 49
Wilde, Oscar 130
Winnett, Ashley 10
Woolworths 160-161

Zen philosophy 55

Join the Institute of Managers and Leaders

If you – like us – believe that Leadership Matters, we'd love you to join the Institute as a member.

The Institute of Managers and Leaders (Australia and New Zealand) offers memberships to all leaders and aspiring leaders. You can join as an Affiliate Member while studying at university and chart your course towards leadership. Or you can join as a Chartered Manager – the international gold-standard in management and leadership excellence.

Contact the Institute and make your mark as a manager or a leader.

Call the Member Services Centre on
1300 IML ANZ (1300 661 061)
email **membership@managersandleaders.com.au**
or visit **www.managersandleaders.com.au**

Printed in May 2019
by Rotomail Italia S.p.A., Vignate (MI) - Italy